To Rhonda,

A woman of grace, beauty and brilliance!

Thank you for understanding.

May we walk arm-in-arm one day on my only street in Paris.

With affection,

Elaine Sciolino

THE
ONLY
STREET
IN
PARIS

La Seduction:
How the French Play the Game of Life

Persian Mirrors:
The Elusive Face of Iran

The Outlaw State: Saddam Hussein's Quest
for Power and the Gulf Crisis

THE
ONLY STREET
IN PARIS

Life on the
Rue des Martyrs

ELAINE SCIOLINO

W. W. NORTON & COMPANY

INDEPENDENT PUBLISHERS SINCE 1923

NEW YORK   LONDON

For information about permission to reproduce selections from this book,
write to Permissions, W. W. Norton & Company, Inc.,
500 Fifth Avenue, New York, NY 10110

For information about special discounts for bulk purchases, please contact
W. W. Norton Special Sales at specialsales@wwnorton.com or 800-233-4830

Photographs by Gabriela Sciolino Plump

Manufacturing by RR Donnelley Westford
Book design by Barbara Bachman
Production manager: Louise Mattarelliano

ISBN 978-0-393-24237-9

W. W. Norton & Company, Inc.
500 Fifth Avenue, New York, N.Y. 10110
www.wwnorton.com

W. W. Norton & Company Ltd.
Castle House, 75/76 Wells Street, London W1T 3QT

1 2 3 4 5 6 7 8 9 0

IN MEMORY OF

GAETANO "TOM"

SCIOLINO

and

ANTHONY "TONY THE

FOOD KING" SCIOLINO

PARIS. — Rue des Martyrs

ND Phot

CONTENTS

LIST OF
ILLUSTRATIONS

T H E

O N L Y

S T R E E T

I N

P A R I S

THE
PERFECT
STREET

. . .

The rue des Martyrs is the center of France.

— SIOBHAN MLACAK,
NEIGHBORHOOD PHOTOGRAPHER

The rue des Martyrs is the center of the world.

—LILIANE KEMPF, RESIDENT OF
THE RUE DES MARTYRS FOR FIFTY YEARS

SOME PEOPLE LOOK AT THE RUE DES MARTYRS AND see a street. I see stories.

For me, it is the last real street in Paris, a half-mile celebration of the city in all its diversity—its rituals and routines, its permanence and transience, its quirky old family-owned shops and pretty young boutiques. This street represents what is left of the intimate, human side of Paris.

I can never be sad on the rue des Martyrs. There are espressos to drink, baguettes to sniff, corners to discover, people to meet. There's a showman who's been running a transvestite cabaret for

PARIS. — *Rues Notre-Dame-de-Lorette et des Martyrs*

ND. Phot.

more than half a century, a woman who repairs eighteenth-century mercury barometers, and an owner of a century-old bookstore with a passion for left-wing philosophers. There are merchants who seduce me with their gastronomic passions: artichokes so young they can be served raw, a Côtes du Rhône so smooth it could be a fine Burgundy, a Mont d'Or cheese so creamy it is best eaten with a spoon. The small food shops on the lower end have no doors. That makes them cold in winter, hot in summer, damp when it rains, and inviting no matter what the weather.

The shopkeepers enforce a culinary camaraderie that has helped me discover my inner Julia Child. What Child wrote in *My Life in France* resonates here as in no other place: "The Parisian grocers insisted that I interact with them personally. If I wasn't willing to take the time to get to know them and their wares, then I would not go home with the freshest legumes or cuts of meat in my basket. They certainly made me work for my supper—but, oh, what suppers!"

Like Julia, I interact personally. I work for my supper. I caress tomatoes, inspect veal chops, sniff ripe Camembert, sample wild boar charcuterie, and go wobbly over buttery brioche. The foodsellers watch, bemused. I have been introduced to a sweet turnip with yellow stripes named "Ball of Gold"; I have been taught to liberate a raw almond from its skin by slamming it into a wall. Sometimes I even pretend to be Julia, who, like me, spoke strongly American-accented French. (I never, ever try to imitate her voice—an odd blend of shrillness and warmth—or her chortling laugh. That I leave to Meryl Streep.)

The rue des Martyrs does not belong to monumental Paris. You won't find it in most Paris guidebooks. About a mile northeast of the place de l'Opéra and half a mile south of the Sacré-Coeur Basilica, it cuts through former working-class neighborhoods of the Ninth and Eighteenth Arrondissements. It lacks the grandeur of the Champs-Élysées and the elegance of Saint-Germain. Yet it has made history. On this street, the patron saint of France was beheaded, the Jesuits took their first vows, and the ritual of communicating with the dead was codified. It was here that Edgar Degas and Pierre-Auguste Renoir painted circus acrobats, Émile Zola situated a lesbian dinner club in his novel *Nana*, and François Truffaut filmed scenes from *The 400 Blows*. The rue des Martyrs is mentioned in Gustave Flaubert's *Sentimental Education*, arguably the most influential French novel of the nineteenth century, and in Guy de Maupassant's *Bel-Ami*, a scandalous tale of opportunism and corruption. More recently, Pharrell Williams, Kanye West, and the band Phoenix came here to record songs at a state-of-the-art music studio.

The rue des Martyrs is not long—about half a mile, no longer than the stretch of New York's Fifth Avenue between Rockefeller Center and Central Park. But its activity is much more concentrated: nearly two hundred small shops and restaurants are packed into its storefronts. Although it is wide enough for cars to park on one side, it is so narrow that people living in apartments facing the street know the comings and goings of residents and shopkeepers just across the way. There is the old woman who stands on her balcony for a cigarette each morning, the man who washes his windows every Tuesday, and the young couple who open their shutters and play loud music before going to work.

Early each morning, a respectable-looking young woman heads to her job at a massage parlor that everyone knows offers more than massages, while nannies from far-off places like Mali and Cameroon drop off children at a day-care center hidden inside a courtyard. Late each afternoon, as residents begin returning home from work, an elderly woman sings to herself, filling the sidewalks with childish tones of "la, la, la, la," while a battered musician with missing teeth and a guitar strapped on his back wanders in and out of shops, displaying varying degrees of coherence.

Every Saturday morning, I sit at the café at No. 8 and face the rue des Martyrs to watch the show. The actors perform on six mini-stages on the other side of the street: my greengrocer and my favorite cheese shop and my butcher at No. 3, my fallback cheese shop and my fish store at No. 5, and the front of my supermarket, where an itinerant chair caner sets up at No. 9. I order a *café crème*. Mohamed (a.k.a. Momo) Allili, the day manager, doesn't mind when I bring a sugared brioche from my favorite bakery next door. This café serves as my personal salon, where neighbors and merchants come and tell stories of the street's history and its transformation over the years.

The rue des Martyrs has managed to retain the feel of a small village despite the globalization and gentrification rolling over Paris like a bulldozer without brakes. As an outsider, I am part of the forces of modernization that threaten to dismantle the street's centuries-old community. Yet over time—partly through what I call random acts of meddling, inspired by my journalist's curiosity—I have broken into this tight-knit community. I have built relationships with those who live and work here—not necessarily deep friendships, but attachments created by a shared passion for a discrete geographical space. At first they involved transactions—goods bought and sold—and with enough time, they extended to experiences shared.

It is the tenacity of the small, traditional merchants and artisans that keeps the character of the street intact. Now they know me, and I know them. I've spent so much time on the street that I've learned the landscapes of their lives: their aches and pains, their vacation destinations, the names and ages of their children. I've heard about the family wedding back home in Tunisia and the attempted holdup of the jewelry store by gunmen. I know who takes a long, hot shower every morning and who has a fantasy of meeting the actress Sharon Stone. I know who suffers from diabetes and who secretly dyes his hair.

I know about the merchant whose marriage ended in divorce when he discovered his wife in bed with another man. He went for the lover's throat, spent forty-eight hours in jail, and was given a fine and a one-month suspended sentence for assault.

"What would you do if you found your husband in bed—in your bed—with another woman?" he asked me over coffee. "Wouldn't you react with rage?"

I told him I might kneecap him, Sicilian-style.

I know about the torture Kamel the greengrocer endured when he went home to Tunisia for a sciatica cure. The local healer made deep cuts in Kamel's ankle and back until he touched the sciatic nerve. Then he took a nail with a head the size of a quarter, heated it in charcoal until the head turned red, and seared the cuts. He didn't use anesthesia. The large burns on Kamel's skin healed unevenly. I know this because he lifted his shirt and one of his trouser legs to show me. Somehow, the unconventional treatment worked.

The street is a hothouse of intimacy. Information becomes currency that has value and can be passed around. When I told

Annick, who runs the cheese store at No. 3 with her husband, Yves, that a new merchant had been rude, she told my friend Amélie, who immediately reported the story back to me with 20 percent more color and drama. When I reminded Ezzidine, then the greengrocer at No. 16, that he had promised to take me to the Rungis wholesale food market just outside of Paris, he informed me that he knew I had also asked one of his competitors down the street to do the same. He wasn't angry; he just wanted me to know that he knew.

The feelings of community are strongest among merchants clustered at the bottom of the street, who refer to themselves as "family." Service trumps competition. When the greengrocer at No. 3 ran out of flat green beans, he grabbed some for me from the greengrocer at No. 4, across the street. My pharmacy has female pharmacists who know my daughters and me so well that I often consult them before calling the doctor.

When I needed a seat small enough to fit into a shower after my older daughter, Alessandra, sprained her ankle, I went first to the hardware store at No. 1, then to the variety store at No. 16. Finally, Ezzidine walked me over to Orphée, the sliver of a store selling jewelry and watches at No. 9, across the street, and introduced me to Joseph, the owner. Joseph gave me a chair and told me to bring it back when I no longer needed it.

Acceptance in the "family" comes with privileges but also with a code of conduct: smile and say *bonjour* to every merchant you pass; stop in for a chat even if you're not buying; never, ever be rude. This means I cannot be rushed. It can take thirty minutes to walk a few hundred feet. I confess there are times when I'm not up for small talk, when I try to avoid the shopkeepers by taking a shortcut through the supermarket. But François the

supermarket security guard knows me now; he always smiles and says *bonjour.*

No matter what the day, I never walk alone on the rue des Martyrs. Somehow, I have made the street mine. I say and do things I wouldn't dare say and do anywhere else in Paris.

No one, except my two daughters, makes fun of me.

SEARCHING
FOR HOME

. . .

"It will be dark," she said.

"No, it has good light," he said. "When I was here it was
getting morning sun."

"I never imagined living on the *premier étage.*"

—DIANE JOHNSON, *Le Mariage*

*I*T TOOK ME A DECADE TO GET TO THE RUE DES MAR-
tyrs. I discovered the street shortly after my husband, Andy, and
I moved to Paris with our two daughters, in 2002. The street
became my go-to place on Sunday mornings, when its shops are
open while much of Paris is shut tight. In those days, it was a
relatively unknown alternative to the tourist-clogged Marais. I
called it the "anti-Marais."

I came to Paris as bureau chief for the *New York Times;* Andy
took a job as the only American in a French law firm. We arrived
with a plan to go back home after three years, five years max.
Then Andy passed the French bar exam. Then we wanted Gabriela, our younger daughter, to finish high school. We stayed on
for a sixth year, then a seventh and an eighth.

No longer new expatriates in the first flush of love with France, we became long-term residents with respectable French and mastery of the Paris Métro. Our daughters went off to college in America, and we decided to downsize and leave our sophisticated neighborhood off the rue du Bac, in the Seventh Arrondissement. I wanted the other side of the Seine. I wanted the rue des Martyrs.

In 2010, a year—yes, a year—into the Paris search, an ad for a suspiciously too-good-to-be-true apartment just off the rue des Martyrs popped up on a real estate website. It was on the rue Notre-Dame-de-Lorette a few steps from one of the architectural gems of the Ninth Arrondissement, the wheel-shaped place Saint-Georges. The space was good, the rent reasonable. The real estate agent, who worked next door, told us the building even had a fringe benefit that has become a rarity in Paris: a superb concierge.

All of this was demonstrably true. We met the concierge, Ilda Da Costa, and learned that she was Portuguese-born and lived with her husband in a 650-square-foot apartment off the courtyard. They'd raised their three sons there. For more than three decades, she had watched over the building with a combination of intelligence, rigorous attention to detail, and a sense of humor. She was also cool. She wore slim jeans and sneakers and pulled her hair back in a ponytail.

Alas, the apartment was flawed.

Paris is called the "City of Light," but the dirty little secret is that it is dark most of the year. It is a northern city, on about the same latitude as Seattle. (New York, by contrast, sits on a level with Madrid and Naples.) The apartment was on the *premier étage*: the first floor as the French count it, one floor up in American parlance. Living on the *premier étage* meant coexisting with the demons of darkness.

And there was no elevator. That suggested dark corridors, peeling paint, lead pipes, faulty electrical wiring, and unreliable door locks.

The most serious disincentive was the shop on the ground floor just below the apartment. It was called Pyro Folie's, and it sold fireworks for parties and special-effects material for the stage. Its picture window was decorated with large jars of highly flammable cellulose in a dozen colors.

As a former Washington-based reporter who once wrote about the CIA, I thought I knew a thing or two about uncovering secrets. I launched an investigation of the building. I visited the neighborhood firehouse and the prefecture of police. The police officers and firefighters assured me that they had no records of explosions on file. I interrogated Marie-Ange Roidor, Pyro Folie's manager, who gave me a look that said, "Who is this crazy American? She's probably a vegetarian too."

Celestine Bohlen, my friend and former *New York Times* colleague who lives around the corner, stopped by Pyro Folie's to follow up. She spoke to a young man working there. "He did his best to reassure," she told me. "He said, 'We don't have a nuclear reactor. We've been here thirty-five years. We are grown-ups, sound of mind.'"

Celestine also noted, however, that two rings pierced one of his eyebrows and that he let slip that fireworks are kept in the salesroom on the ground floor (just below the apartment's master bedroom).

That led me to ask a young French friend to consult her father, an admiral who had once been in charge of France's Naval Commandos. He had decades of experience with explosives and land mines, in countries like Chad and Afghanistan.

"Elaine wants to know whether she should move into an apartment above a fireworks store," she told him.

He gave her a stern military look and responded with a question: "Would you live on top of a wasp's nest?"

That should have settled it.

But the outside of the building looked promising. The glossy dark paint on its heavy, wooden outer door had worn away in places, giving it an air of shabby chic. The door had an elaborate wrought-iron *grille* featuring lions, rabbits, birds, and mythical sea monsters. More wrought iron—curved forms over two feet high—anchored each side of the door frame to the ground. Long ago, they had served to protect the building from damage by horse-drawn carriages.

From the moment I stepped into the cobblestoned courtyard, I was no longer thinking about explosions in the middle of the night. I was transported back to the first half of the nineteenth century. There were none of the oversized plastic garbage bins, motorcycles, and bicycles that had cluttered our old building's courtyard. What were once horse stables had been transformed into automobile garages with discreet black wooden doors.

Then I was escorted into the entryway. Before me was an astonishing architectural feature that I would later learn had been designated as a French historical monument: a wide, curving, oval wooden staircase with a rosewood-and-wrought-iron banister and a gold-trimmed runner in two-toned green. The staircase soared in elegance to an oval beveled-glass skylight that opened up to the sun.

The apartment door opened to reveal twelve-foot-high ceilings. The original doors, mirrors, fireplaces, and ceiling moldings were intact. The designs on the moldings were so intricate that they had names: *denticules,* as in teeth; *palmettes,* as in palm leaves; *marguerites,* as in daisies. Light flooded in through eight-and-a-half-foot-high windows—even sunlight!

I knew we were home.

OUR APARTMENT IS NOT, strictly speaking, on the rue des Martyrs. But the street's bounty of merchandise and frenzy of activity are a mere five hundred feet from my front door. I currently count on the rue des Martyrs:

26 restaurants and bistros

3 cabarets and theaters

5 bar-cafés, including a piano bar

5 tea salons

2 supermarkets

13 *traiteurs* and take-out shops

6 greengrocers

3 butchers

13 bakeries and pastry shops

2 fish shops

3 cheese shops

5 chocolate shops

4 wine merchants

21 clothing stores

3 secondhand clothing shops

5 jewelers

7 hairdressers

4 skin-care salons

3 pharmacies

5 opticians

2 florists

3 independent bookstores

5 banks

4 real estate agencies

2 hotels

It doesn't stop there. Add in a church, a high school, a retirement home, a hardware store, a day-care center, a self-service laundry, a recording studio, a mobile phone store. And a locksmith and shoe cobbler, a barometer and gilt frame restorer, a tailor, a musical instrument repairer, and a gay bathhouse called Sauna Mykonos, with a facade like a Greek temple.

Who could ask for anything more?

THE RUE DES MARTYRS STARTS a block south of the place Saint-Georges, at the dirty back wall of a forlorn church that from this perspective looks like a prison. It moves north, mostly one-way with an uphill angle steep enough to force a walker to slow down. It dead-ends at a cross street that takes you to an even steeper climb straight to the Sacré-Coeur Basilica at the top of Montmartre, the highest point of Paris. The rue des Martyrs can be perceived as two streets—or, better, two worlds—divided by a wide boulevard about three-fourths of the way up. The part below belongs to nineteenth-century commercial and financial

Paris, the part above to what was once the village of Montmartre, outside the city limits.

Immediately, in obedience to my journalistic instincts, I wanted to know everything about my new home, and why the rue des Martyrs has retained the feel of a small village. The street jealously guards its secrets: it has no landmarks, no important architecture, no public gardens, nor any stone plaques on the sides of buildings telling you who was born, lived, worked, or died here. But I didn't have to go into reporter mode to seek out the experts who could help. They found me.

The process began at a street fair at the place Saint-Georges. The *place* had recently been renovated, and the volunteer association in the Ninth Arrondissement had decided to celebrate with food, drink, songs, speeches, and guided tours of the historic sites. At the center of the *place* is a defunct fountain with a large bust of Paul Gavarni, a nineteenth-century neighborhood painter and caricaturist. One side of the *place* is dominated by a mansion encrusted with multi-colored marbles and heavy with busts and statues; it is best known as the residence of the nineteenth-century Russian-born queen of kept women known as La Païva. On the other side is an 1873 mansion that houses a library of nineteenth-century French history for scholars, built by the French state for the politician and writer Adolphe Thiers. At the Théâtre Saint-Georges, on the corner, François Truffaut shot scenes for his 1980 film *The Last Metro*.

It was at this street fair that I met Didier Chagnas, a militant cheerleader for the neighborhood. Didier, well into his eighties, sports a scruffy salt-and-pepper beard. His sweater hugged his big belly; his pants were so long that they covered his shoes. His plaid sport coat was much too big and looked as if he had found it at a church sale. (He probably had.)

Didier was holding forth to some twenty people in front of La Païva's mansion. With its stone angels and lions and Gothic and Renaissance-style statues, the mansion is so showy that it was chosen as the setting for the American embassy in the 2006 film *The Da Vinci Code*. Didier said it was conceived as a fancy rental apartment building; later a more luxurious, permanent residence was built for La Païva on the Avenue des Champs-Élysées. At one point Didier wandered off topic and started talking about the rue Notre-Dame-de-Lorette, my street, which runs through the *place*. "I myself have lived in Number 15 since 1975," he said.

"You have? I live in 18!" I said.

"Ah! You have a very beautiful staircase!" he exclaimed.

He took a deep breath and switched topics. Out came my building's history. He called it one of the most beautiful bourgeois houses of the neighborhood. The building was financed by a businessman named Pierre Lemarié and was built in 1837. It had an unusual feature: entrances on two different streets so that horses and horse-drawn carriages could move in and out easily. Didier got so excited that he crossed the line of French politesse. "Could we all go into the courtyard with you?" he asked. "Come on, let's go! Is that okay?"

I hesitated. My husband and I are the only foreigners and non-owners in the building (except for the young renters in the maids' rooms on the sixth floor). That means we doubly do not belong. To lead a gaggle of curiosity-seeking French people into our courtyard could expose me to the wrath of our privacy-conscious neighbors. But this was a day to celebrate. In no time at all, we were parading toward my building.

When we arrived at the door, Didier stopped short. "First, we must appreciate the decorative wrought iron on the wooden door!" he said. So we did.

Then I punched in the door code and we filed into the entry-way. Didier pointed out the friezes with hunting motifs and representations of the star-crossed twelfth-century lovers Héloïse and Abélard that are mounted above two of the inner doors. He said that so many buildings like mine were constructed at the time that friezes had to be mass-produced in plaster molds, sold by the meter, and painted to look like stone.

He took us deep into the courtyard and drew our attention to the original pavement of large square cobblestones and the one-car garages that were once stables for horses. Then he led us into a second, smaller courtyard where a nineteenth-century fountain stands. *Please, please,* I thought. *Please get us through this before one of the neighbors comes out and orders us to leave.* But Didier was just getting warmed up. He said that a famous portrait photographer, Nadar (whose real name was Gaspard-Félix Tournachon), had his studio here at some point in the mid-nineteenth century. "He photographed just about every celebrity," said Didier. Among his subjects, I discovered later, were Hector Berlioz, Sarah Bernhardt, Jacques Offenbach, George Sand, Guy de Maupassant, Édouard Manet, Gustave Doré, Gustave Courbet, Franz Liszt, Richard Wagner, Charles Baudelaire, Victor Hugo, and Jules Verne.

Didier went on: "I don't want to say something stupid, but I believe that Jules Verne lived here." Jules Verne? I live in the same building as the man who wrote *Around the World in Eighty Days*? (I have never found evidence to confirm this, but what a delicious fantasy.)

Most remarkable, Didier said, are the unique staircase and skylight in the front entrance, which are oval, not round as are others of the Charles X building era. People in our group nodded solemnly, as if they knew everything about Charles X, the small-minded, ultra-conservative king of France from 1824 until 1830. His most important legacy was that he had an architectural style named after him. I had no choice but to open the inner door so that our group could carry out an inspection.

At this point, a thin, middle-aged man in our group took over. He didn't introduce himself, but I soon learned who he was: Thierry Cazaux, an executive with the American investment firm Cantor Fitzgerald by day and the unofficial historian and passionate promoter of the neighborhood at lunchtime, on week-ends, and by night. He explained that there had once been a plan to install an elevator inside the oval stairwell and he had been part of the cabal to stop it.

I later learned that Jean-Pierre Gauffier, the preservationist-crusader who owns the apartment above mine, was its leader. He waged an eight-year battle against the elevator. The pro-elevator lobby on the upper floors argued that Gauffier's campaign was unfair, as he lived on a lower floor and had only two flights to climb.

In 2008, the French government designated elements of the building as "historical monuments" because of their authenticity and exceptional quality. That included not only the staircase, the stairwell's black-and-white stone floor, and the skylight, but also the cobblestone-paved courtyard and the building's three cov-ered passageways. That means they cannot be tampered with and are protected by law.

Every once in a while, Jean-Pierre told me, the keyhole of his front door is packed tight with chewing gum—a silent guerrilla operation from one of the pro-elevatorists, he assumes. He can usually dig it out with a hairpin, but sometimes he has to call a locksmith to get it unstuck.

By this time, I was so deep into the exercise that I was tempted to invite the group in for coffee. But in my upper-crust former neighborhood on the other side of town I would never, ever have brought strangers home. And I couldn't remember if I had made the bed. So Didier, Thierry, and the group said their thank-yous and good-byes. One middle-aged man stayed behind. He wore round tortoiseshell glasses, a corduroy sport coat, jeans, and loafers, and he carried a small green backpack. With a sweet smile, he said his name was Michel Güet, that he was retired, and that he knew a thing or two about the history of the neighborhood.

"May I offer to show you around?" he asked, oh so politely.

I'm from the tough West Side of Buffalo and came to Paris via New York City, Chicago, Beirut, Tehran, and Baghdad. When a stranger offers to show me around, I normally ignore him and keep walking, fast. But it was broad daylight, and I was at the edge of my neighborhood fair with hundreds of people. I half-smiled and mumbled something like "Oh, yes, that would be nice." Then I excused myself to get on with my day.

Fortunately for me, we would soon meet again.

IS FISH
NECESSARY?

...

I closed my eyes and inhaled the rising perfume.
Then I lifted a forkful of fish to my mouth, took a bite,
and chewed slowly. The flesh of the sole was delicate,
with a light but distinct taste of the ocean that
blended marvelously with the browned butter. It was a
morsel of perfection.

—Julia Child, *My Life in France*

*W*HEN LA POISSONNERIE BLEUE, AT NO. 5 RUE DES
Martyrs, went out of business, it was more than the closing of a
shop. It was the end of a family business and the destruction of a
web of neighborhood relationships with the fishmongers. Collective horror set in that the street was losing its soul, along with its
sole. I shared in the general dismay.

La Poissonnerie Bleue had an awning the color of the sea
when a sun-filled sky turns it the warmest of blues. It had been in
business for more than a half century. Marc Briolay, the owner,
had started working there in 1978, when he was still a teenager.

He and his wife, Évelyne, had raised their two children in the 950-square-foot rental apartment upstairs.

They built La Poissonnerie Bleue into a family-run operation. Their daughter, Justine, greeted customers out front. Their son, Thomas, scaled, gutted, and filleted in the back. Marc made change and worked the credit card machine. Évelyne kept the books. But now business was bad. Running a fish store is expensive, and Marc, I suspect, was more artisan than businessman. Revenues fell in 2011 and again in 2012.

Beneath the calm surface, a war waged over the shop's broken ice machine—a longstanding dispute between Marc and his landlord over who would pay the 8,000 euros to repair it. Every fish shop needs large quantities of shaved ice. So Marc was forced to buy his own, an expense as extravagant as it was necessary.

That was not all. The walls, the ceiling, the refrigerator—they all needed work. Then there was the problem of the balcony. The Briolays claimed that a piece of it had once fallen on Thomas's head. At some point, with these issues unresolved, the Briolays began withholding rent. When they owed the landlord 50,000 euros, he ordered them out.

In the United States, when a neighborhood merchant closes after so many years, there is often a ritual to mark the event. A fire sale, perhaps, or a going-away party. In France, there is a tendency to pretend it isn't happening. So the announcement came in faint and barely legible writing on the "Suggestion of the Day" chalkboard that hung in front of the shop: "The fish store will close for good on October 31, 2012. Thank you. The Management."

Because Marc refused to discuss the impending closure, Évelyne, who rarely ventured into the shop, came to do the talking.

"There are things I can't pay for," she confessed. "I have no shame in saying it."

To any customer willing to listen, she said, "This is going to kill the bottom of the rue des Martyrs! This is a little village. Parents bring their kids here to teach them about food."

Her greatest fear was that a shoe store would move in. The more she talked, the darker her predictions: "If there's no fish shop, the neighborhood is dead!"

Everyone had an opinion about what could happen next, and all of the opinions were negative. Maybe the Carrefour supermarket next door would break down the walls and expand. Maybe yet another cheese shop or bakery would take over. No one had much hope that another fishmonger would move in.

"Where will we go for fish?" one customer lamented. "Picard?" Picard is a national all-frozen-food supermarket chain with an outlet around the corner. Its frozen red mullet is half the price of the fresh counterpart at La Poissonnerie Bleue, but Picard is viewed with disdain by traditional French cooks. The dirty little secret is that some Picard fish is *pas mal,* which in French doesn't mean "not bad"; it actually means pretty good, only no one was admitting that in this crisis.

There was a smaller fresh-fish store several blocks up the street, but for residents of the lower rue des Martyrs, that was a world away. "Too far, too far," said Yves Chataigner, who runs a cheese shop with his wife Annick, at No. 3 rue des Martyrs. "It might as well be New York."

It wasn't only that. The distant shop offered less choice, was owned by a chain, and employed fishmongers who didn't bother to learn their clients' names or fish preferences. (When I asked them for their reaction to the impending closure of their main competition below, they replied with Gallic shrugs.) It was also up the hill, an incline that gets steeper as the street moves north, toward Montmartre.

"How will all the old grandmas get their fish?" asked Valérie Levin, the baker's wife across the street.

Since this is France, where people hold the government responsible for just about anything that goes wrong, Valérie insisted that city hall should guarantee access to fresh fish. "The authorities have an obligation to put a fish store here, a civic obligation," she said. She circulated a petition demanding a fishmonger. Two hundred people signed.

Not everyone was sad. Some thought La Poissonnerie Bleue was old-fashioned on a street beginning to turn hip. The presentation was predictable, not innovative. "The 'look' of the fish is not sexy," said one customer. "There's nothing to astonish me, to take my breath away."

I asked Jacques Bravo, then the local mayor of the Ninth Arrondissement, if he could help the Briolays. Each of Paris's twenty administrative units, or *arrondissements*, has its own mayor. Although these mini-mayors report to the head mayor of Paris, they have considerable authority over their own domains.

Bravo's wife had rushed home a few days before to tell him that something terrible was happening to La Poissonnerie Bleue, that the entire street was talking about it. Bravo was resigned to the inevitable. The next Sunday morning, he turned up on the rue des Martyrs in a gray cashmere scarf and a pin-striped suit with a red rosette pinned to the left lapel designating him as an *officier* of the Legion of Honor. He shook a lot of hands before delivering the bad news. He had been presented just the day before with many delicate details about what had gone wrong. "I love this family," he said. "They're very honorable. But it will be impossible to save them." Nevertheless, he had solidarity with fish, if not with the fishmonger. He promised to try to find a replacement for Marc, maybe a young couple with a love of fish and a hunger for work. He cited the protection of the rue des Martyrs under the Paris Local Urbanism Plan law of 2006, which safeguards small independent artisanal businesses. "There will be a butcher here. There will be a baker here. There will be a cheesemonger here. And maybe, just maybe, there will be a fishmonger here. I'm a marathoner. And I can always speed up at the end."

But he acknowledged that it was difficult to find fresh-fish sellers these days. Fish is a hard profession, with a high overhead. The trend in recent years is for fishmongers to set up stands in open-air markets that travel around to different neighborhoods.

In its final days, the atmosphere inside the fish store became tense. The full-time employee in charge of the smoked salmon counter was Joël Vicogne, who'd started working there when he was sixteen. He also happened to be the son of the landlord, who had once run the shop himself, in partnership with an uncle. Where did Joël's loyalties lie? Was he a spy for his father? Plotting a takeover?

Joël, now well into middle age, had no intention of assuming the job of neighborhood fishmonger. "Fish is too tough," he explained. "You have to be at the wholesale market at two, three in the morning. You have to be on your feet in rubber boots eight hours a day. You don't get enough vacation."

I wanted to toast the Briolays on their last day, so I arrived at the store on October 31 with plastic cups and two bottles of champagne. But Marc had thwarted my plan by shutting down three days earlier. There had been no toasts, no tears, no good-byes. Just the clang of metal shutters closing the shop for the last time.

I took the news hard. No matter how busy the shop, how long the line stretched onto the sidewalk, there had always been time at La Poissonnerie Bleue to talk about fish. I learned there that an ugly-faced variety of ocean perch called *sébaste* is excellent stuffed with shallots or fennel and baked whole; that fresh cod works well with pesto; that red mullet is not too delicate to fillet and sauté. Justine, Marc's daughter, had shared her secret recipe for linguine with shrimp, fish quenelles, and a sauce of butter, white wine, and shallots. Marc routinely threw a lemon and a bunch of fresh parsley into my bag and shaved two or three euros off the bill. I had felt like more than just a customer.

Soon after La Poissonnerie Bleue closed, a fancy chocolate and caramel shop opened a few blocks to the north. It was a very un–rue des Martyrs event, with an invitation-only opening day, a red carpet, potted trees at the entrance, and two press agents to answer questions.

Makoto Ishii, the young Japanese manager, dressed in designer black, offered the guests champagne and an endless supply of chocolates. He told me how much he and his wife had liked the rue des Martyrs the first time they had visited, more than a decade ago.

"We got off the Métro and began to walk up the street," he said. "There in front of us in the distance was the Sacré-Coeur Basilica. It was love at first sight. We never left."

They moved into an apartment on the street and later opened the chocolate shop next door.

Somehow, our conversation turned to fish and we agreed that the departure of the Briolay family represented the end of an era.

"There is a missing piece," I said.

"The neighborhood needs fish," replied Makoto. "Maybe I should take over the fish store."

"What? I thought you were a chocolate expert," I said. "You know fish?"

"Of course."

"How do you know fish?"

"I'm Japanese."

Of course.

Months later, the old fish shop was still shuttered. The sign for La Poissonnerie Bleue still hung outside, a painful reminder of what had been lost.

HIDDEN IN
PLAIN SIGHT

...

Paris ... is loath to surrender itself to people who
are in a hurry; it belongs to the dreamers, to those
capable of amusing themselves in its streets without
regard to time when urgent business requires their
presence elsewhere.

—JULIEN GREEN, *Paris*

I HAD FORGOTTEN ALL ABOUT MICHEL GÜET, THE MAN
I encountered at the end of the impromptu group visit to my
building. Then I bumped into him a few weeks later, outside an
all-volunteer community center that ran a bistro at lunchtime. He
was leading a group of retirees on a free tour of the neighborhood. He asked if someday soon I'd like to go on a walk with him
on the rue des Martyrs. *Pourquoi pas?* Why not?

Michel was born in the neighborhood and is passionate about
its past. We met on the front steps of the Notre-Dame-de-Lorette
Church—a fitting start, as he was baptized here.

I hadn't expected a lesson quite like this one. He quickly
assumed the air of a high school geology teacher, launching into

a lecture on the sedimentary rocks under our feet. They formed tens of millions of years ago, when this part of France was underwater, he said, and the walls and pillars of the church were built from this cheap and plentiful stone. To prove the point, he pointed to fossils and shells embedded in the pillars, like tiny jewels of nature.

"You see, here you have a perfect photograph of the bottom of the sea forty or fifty million years ago!" he said. "And to think that we bipeds are not even six million years old. It makes us humble inhabitants of our planet, no?"

I was eager to move forward a few million years. Michel obliged, sort of, and we walked to the back of the church to begin our uphill journey on the rue des Martyrs. He told me that in the Middle Ages, this area was part of a vast swamp. By the fourteenth century, the swamp had been drained and canals built. In the eighteenth century, the street was both residential and commercial, filled with dance halls, cabarets, and more than two dozen small inns, many of which doubled as brothels. Little survives now from that era. Most buildings date from a boom that accompanied prosperity in the first half of the nineteenth century.

The street became the physical spine of the neighborhood, the route between the financial world of the Grands Boulevards and the nightlife of Montmartre. It was built to be *populaire*— solid, unpretentious, working-class, poised between respectability and bohemia.

In the latter part of the nineteenth century, Napoleon III tasked his master city planner, Baron Georges-Eugène Haussmann, with wiping out overcrowded, disease-ridden neighborhoods of Paris in the name of progress. Haussmann replaced twisting, narrow streets and alleyways that had existed for centuries with straight, wider streets and boulevards. The rue des Martyrs was mostly spared. Only a handful of its present structures, uniform five-story buildings with white stone facades and narrow wrought-iron balconies, are considered Haussmannian.

What remains is charming architectural chaos, a hodgepodge of styles and building materials. Some structures have five stories, others only three. Some have been topped with an extra floor or two, adding space but not elegance. Some windows have been enlarged, some not. Some doors and entrances have been replaced with banal metal, some maintained in their original wood with wrought-iron work. Look hard enough, and you can find creativity: brick, ceramic tile, flourishes of Art Nouveau and Art Deco. "We are in a mosaic of memory," Michel said. "I can never pretend to know everything."

Walking on the street with him is a journey into his own personal history. We stopped at the first corner on the right. As a schoolboy, Michel stood on this spot and watched as the supermarket–variety store at No. 7, across the street, went up in flames. "It looked like a giant barbecue," he said. I told him I love this corner for another reason. The rue des Martyrs has no museums or private art galleries. But this corner has one of the most remarkable pieces of street art in Paris: two large advertising murals, one above the other on a wall at No. 10, painted more than a century ago. Long hidden from view, they were rediscovered by chance during construction work. Because they had been protected from sunlight and rain, they are nearly perfectly preserved.

A 1909 mural advertising Ripolin paint is on top. It shows three painters in white coats and straw hats, one in front of another, each holding a paintbrush and a small can of paint. The first is painting the wall; each of the others paints the coat of the painter in front of him. A 1911 mural below advertises Bénédictine with the image of a bottle of the herbal liqueur sitting on a tray. For now, the murals are barely visible behind a protective translucent covering. Crude graffiti scars the Bénédictine ad. They have received official "historic monument" status, but the 150,000 euros or so it would take to restore and protect them is not there.

Michel pointed out the elementary school on the rue Hippolyte-Lebas. "You know who went to this school besides me?" he asked. "François Truffaut!" Truffaut had lived on the rue de Navarin just off the rue des Martyrs, and he set his semiautobiographical black-and-white debut feature film, *The 400 Blows* (1959), in the neighborhood he knew so intimately. Truffaut cast the fourteen-year-old Jean-Pierre Léaud in the film as Antoine Doinel, an independent-minded teenager branded as a troublemaker by all the adults in his life. Antoine lives with his mother and stepfather in a cramped walk-up on the lower part of the rue des Martyrs. In one scene, his mother takes him home from school past the bakery on the corner with rue Manuel; in another, he and his best friend are seen walking inside the Cité Malesherbes, a private residential enclave whose iron gates open onto the rue des Martyrs. In early 2014, a plaque was erected at No. 33 rue de Navarin to celebrate the building where Truffaut spent his childhood and the neighborhood where he made the film, one of the first of the French New Wave.

"This building is interesting, with its second-floor balcony—we're in the 1840s here," Michel said as we passed No. 26. "And look at the ironwork on the door—it's Abélard and Héloïse, and we're in the Romantic period. Across the street"—No. 25—"we have neoclassicism with fake Corinthian columns. That building with the bakery," he noted, and I looked over at No. 26, "dates from 1895, and all those decorations on the facade are just to show off. The building just across the street"—we had now moved on to No. 23—"is a vision in sobriety."

As we stood in front of the sushi shop at No. 32, Michel told me to look at the buildings across the street and down toward the Notre-Dame-de-Lorette Church. "We are seeing the rue des Martyrs exactly as it was in 1840," he said.

To prepare for my tour with Michel, I had done some research on my own; I wanted to show my stuff. I suggested we turn left, onto the rue de Navarin. At No. 9, I pointed out a Gothic Revival house that looks like a miniature cathedral. "Didn't it used to be a brothel?" I said. Across the street, I added, the Hôtel Amour has erotic photographs in rooms that can be rented by the week, by the day, or for "nooners" (noon to three p.m., for about one hundred euros). Michel raised an eyebrow as if to suggest that the rate seemed rather pricey.

The hotel is so cool that its restaurant has offerings like lobster sandwiches, eggs Benedict, and gluten-free carrot cake. All its wines are made with organically grown grapes and, according to the menu, "a lot of love." Its exterior briefly appeared in a commercial for Love Story, Chloé's orange-blossom-and-jasmine-based perfume. French actress Clémence Poésy, dressed in ivory-hued mousseline, floats through a romantic Paris night under the spell of a visibly smitten beau. When morning comes, she dumps him. Meanwhile, "Mi Amor," sung by Vanessa Paradis, plays in the background.

"This is a modern, rock'n'roll, secret woman," said actress-director Mélanie Laurent, who filmed the commercial—and lives in the neighborhood. "And most of all, this is a free woman."

As we walked up the left side of the rue des Martyrs, I told Michel to slow down. "The Sacré-Coeur is about to appear," I said. We caught a glimpse of a small dome on the left. Then we stopped at the corner of the rue Manuel, where the large central dome and a second small dome came into view, chalky white against a blue sky.

Émile Zola, who lived in the neighborhood while Sacré-Coeur was being built, was among those who hated its design and its scale. One of the characters in his novel *Paris*, an *abbé* named Pierre Froment, describes it as "a citadel of the absurd that dominates, insults, and threatens Paris." From our vantage point, however, Sacré-Coeur looked neither absurd nor threatening. "This is the moment of magic," I said. "The street belongs to me."

"To us," said Michel, smiling.

"Didn't Henry Miller turn Sacré-Coeur into a sex object?" I asked. Neither of us knew exactly what the American novelist had written about the basilica when he lived in Paris. I looked it up later and sent the passage from Miller's 1936 memoir-novel *Black Spring* to Michel: "And then suddenly, presto! all is changed. Suddenly the street opens wide its jaws and there, like a still white dream, like a dream embedded in stone, the Sacré-Coeur rises up. A late afternoon and the heavy whiteness of it is stifling. A heavy, somnolent whiteness, like the belly of a jaded woman."

We continued our journey. Most of the rue des Martyrs is treeless. It seems that tree roots interfere with the dense underground network of pipes and electrical cables, although at two short stretches, the sidewalks widen to allow space for a few small plane trees. There aren't many leaves to clean up in fall—but not many birds either, except pigeons.

UNTIL THE MID-NINETEENTH CENTURY, when side streets
cut asphalt gashes through what had once been vast gardens, the
rue des Martyrs had the feel of the countryside. Today, casual
observers would never know that some of the front doors along
the street—most open only with a digital code—hide exquisite
private gardens. Looking through an iron gate at Nos. 41–47, we
could see part of a courtyard and a big central garden framed by
elegant apartment buildings.

Higher up the street is the gated Cité Malesherbes, one of the
most charming private streets in Paris. It begins at the rue des
Martyrs, then angles left and exits on the rue Victor-Massé. One
building was once a maternity hospital and, before abortion
became legal in France, in 1975, a place where women could
safely and secretly terminate their pregnancies. Another building
houses the Jean-Jaurès Foundation, named after the founder of
modern French socialism. The Cité's wrought-iron *grille* is not
locked during the day, but a caretaker sits as a watchdog to keep
away the riffraff.

I kept moving north, but at the street's juncture with two
major boulevards, Rochechouart and Clichy, Michel stopped. He
seemed surprised that I wanted to go to Montmartre.

"I rarely venture there," he said. "I don't know it well."

"Well, I know a few things about it—so let's go!" I said.

Like many people in the neighborhood, Michel thinks of the
rue des Martyrs as two streets—one in the Ninth, where he and
I live, and the other uphill and to the north, in the "village" of
Montmartre, in the Eighteenth. The two areas were divided by
history. In the 1780s, Louis XVI ordered the wall of the *fermiers-
généraux* (farmers-general) to be built around the Paris city lim-

its, not as a defensive fortification but as a revenue raiser for the state. The farmers-general had nothing to do with agriculture; they were a group of financiers appointed by the king to collect taxes and customs duties on all goods entering the city, including salt, food, wine, cider, tobacco, coal, firewood, and building materials. A series of large tollhouses were built, including one at the point where the rue des Martyrs hit the city limits.

Montmartre functioned as an independent commune until 1860, when the wall came down and Paris grew. It expanded from thirteen to thirty square miles, from twelve to twenty arrondissements, and from 1.1 million to 1.7 million inhabitants. Montmartre was among the towns and villages swallowed up by the city. For eight more years, the chaussée des Martyrs, the physical extension of the rue des Martyrs in the newly created Eighteenth Arrondissement, kept its identity. Then *"chaussée"* became *"rue"* and the two parts of the street became one, if in name only.

These days, the two parts are divided by a noisy four-lane thoroughfare with parking lanes and a median strip (where the wall once stood) wide enough for trees, park benches, bicycle lanes, and public toilets. Depending on traffic and traffic lights, it can take a minute or two to cross this physical, geographical, administrative, psychological, and auditory barrier.

The name of the broad thoroughfare itself changes where it crosses the rue des Martyrs. The boulevard de Rochechouart, to the right, is lined with cheap tourist shops. The boulevard de Clichy, to the left, bears witness to the seedy remnants of Pigalle, with its peep shows and sex shops. The Moulin Rouge (it really does look like a *moulin rouge,* or red windmill) still attracts busloads of tourists—many of whom come not for dinner and a floor show but only to take photos. "The sex shops and nightclubs on the boulevard create a barrier," Christophe Thibaudeau, the manager of the Daniel Féau real estate agency, once told me. "My clients ask for one or the other part of the rue des Martyrs—but never both."

When my neighbor Thierry Cazaux wrote a book on the street, he ended it at the border with the Eighteenth. For him, that's a world away. "It's the other side of the boulevards," he said, as if that explained everything. "The wall hasn't been there for a hundred and fifty years, but there are still two streets—one in Paris, the other not."

People on the other side feel the same way. When I asked Raymond Lansoy, the editor of a small monthly magazine on Montmartre, whether a legendary restaurant had been on the Ninth or Eighteenth side of the rue des Martyrs, he feigned annoyance: "You are sweet, Elaine, but from time to time you get on my nerves! You are not in the Eighteenth, you are in Montmartre."

He said some residents of Montmartre rarely go south of the boulevard, and when they do, they say, "I'm going down to Paris."

Even my husband jokes that I am stretching things in making the street one. "By now you must know that no one but you considers it one street," he said as we dodged traffic and bicyclists to cross the boulevard one Sunday.

Having persuaded Michel Güet to go into Montmartre, I pointed out La Fourmi, a café-bistro on the northeast corner. I like it because you can sit on stools at the zinc bar and thereby pay lower prices than if you sit at a table. We then walked on the stretch of street with the transvestite cabaret, the music hall for rent, and the bar whose goal is never to close.

At the corner of the rue des Abbesses, on our left, we could see the edge of the place des Abbesses, made famous in Jean-Pierre Jeunet's 2001 French cult film *Amélie*. The Abbesses microneighborhood has attracted cool chain stores with over-priced clothing; cool bistros that offer hot dogs, bagels, and brunch; and cool couples crowding the narrow sidewalks with cool babies in cool strollers. Abbesses has become one of Paris's tourist destinations. It could be in prettified Brooklyn, which makes the contrast with the authentic, unrenovated upper rue des Martyrs more dramatic.

"This is not my world," said Michel.

The rue des Martyrs dead-ends at a juncture with the rue La Vieuville and an art gallery that has kept the sign of an older shop: *"Papiers Peints"*—wallpaper. If we had jogged to the right here, we could have joined waves of tourists and continued north up steep stretches and staircases to Sacré-Coeur. Instead, we turned back.

On our way down, we stopped at an upscale private retire-ment home that gives this part of the street an air of respectabil-ity. "I've heard it has a beautiful garden," I said to Michel. "I wrote a letter asking for permission to see it and never got an answer. Let's go in and see what happens."

We entered a quiet lobby and approached the receptionist, a serious-looking woman of about forty. She was polite and firm: this was private property and she could not allow us into the garden.

Michel and I went into seduction mode. I introduced myself by name and said I was a longtime American resident of Paris researching the rue des Martyrs. Michel explained that he had spent his entire life in the neighborhood. When the receptionist heard that my first name was Elaine, she said she was called Elena

Da Cunha. Soon, she and I were discussing her Portuguese roots, my Sicilian ones, the salted dried cod of our childhoods, and how destiny had brought us together. Elena led us into the garden, a deep oval expanse lined with white lilac trees and planted with tulips and daffodils. Michel and I sat on one of the benches listening to the quiet, pleased with our victory.

SINCE THEN, I HAVE LEARNED that for those who can get beyond the walls and gates, there is more, much more, to discover about the look of the rue des Martyrs than what can be seen from the sidewalk. My key to a tour of the Cité Malesherbes was Thierry Cazaux, the cultured Ninth Arrondissement insider who had contributed information about my building to Didier Chagnas's group tour. Thierry grew up at No. 8 Cité Malesherbes and still lives there with his ailing father. He has even written a short book about it (and another about the rue des Martyrs). I wrote him several times asking to visit, and he always put me off with an exquisite excuse. Then, for once, I must have said the right thing. He gave me a tour of the Cité Malesherbes.

Inside the gate, the small street is lined with townhouses, most of them private residences with landmark status. No. 9 was built with artists in mind, with a two-story, 150-square-foot atelier; Théodore Rousseau, the champion of the Barbizon school, had painted at this address. No. 12 has a neoclassical look, with sculpted stone masks and long garlands of fruits and flowers on the facade, wrought-iron balconies, and a garden of more than three hundred square feet. No. 20 shows off an Art Nouveau spiral staircase enclosed in glass, making it visible from the outside.

The facade of No. 11 is adorned in riotous color: its ceramic plaques and enameled lava stone have been painted with miniature reproductions of the art of Paris's Saint-Vincent-de-Paul Church.

No. 8, Thierry's house, was built in the 1860s. Its parlor could be a museum, or at least the set for a film about the late-nineteenth-century Parisian bourgeoisie. (I call it a parlor and not a living room because it doesn't look livable.) The decor dates from a century ago, or so it seems: oil paintings covering the walls, almost up to the ceiling; a pastel-colored rug with a floral pattern laid over worn gray wall-to-wall carpeting; uncomfortable, horsehair-filled chairs. We sat there in semidarkness, without artificial light, until Thierry said he had something else to show me. He led me through the dining room and out a back door into a large garden with a round table and chairs at its center. It was here, he said, that he did his best work.

I discovered another special house while food shopping one Sunday morning. Pauline Véron, then deputy mayor of the Ninth Arrondissement, was campaigning to become mayor: shaking hands, kissing babies, listening to complaints. She introduced me to a woman in her eighties with impeccable makeup and blond hair pulled into a poufy bun. The woman's clothes showed her curves to their best advantage; "dolled up" would be the old-fashioned way to describe her. She was talking nonstop.

"She is the best expert you could ever find on the rue des Martyrs," Pauline said when she brought us together. "Her house is a hidden jewel. Maybe she will invite you over one day."

That day was today. "Follow me!" the woman commanded, so I began trailing someone whom I had just met and whose name I didn't know.

We stopped at No. 46, the entrance next to Rose Bakery, a British-style bakery, café, and food shop specializing in organic vegetable tarts, scones, and carrot cake. When the place opened, in 2002, it became the best-known destination on the street. It made South African–born Rose Carrarini world-famous: she wrote cookbooks and opened branches in Hong Kong, New York, Tokyo, London, and Seoul.

The woman punched in her digital code to unlock the outer door. We walked through a narrow entrance into a courtyard and garden. A staircase at the back ended at another door, which she opened to reveal an unexpected space: a second, secret garden landscaped with trees and rosebushes. A small, three-story building stood at the end of a path to the left. It had been built 150 years earlier as an artist's studio; the woman and her husband bought it a century later, tripled it in size, and made it home.

She invited me to sit in a large dining room with open windows facing the garden. Then, finally, she told me her name: Liliane Kempf. She was a Spanish-language teacher married to Bertrand, a computer specialist; both were retired. She served me a large slice of homemade blueberry tart and a glass of orange juice; she seemed too eager to talk to spend time making coffee.

She told stories about the rue des Martyrs in the old days, when itinerant merchants sold fruits and vegetables from hand carts they pulled up the street and a dairy shop ladled fresh milk out of huge metal cans. She said her late aunt remembered horse-drawn carriages ferrying pedestrians uphill during winter, when it was too slippery to walk. My favorite story was the one she told about an unknown waif of a street singer, Édith Giovanna Gassion. Poor, thin, and only four feet, eight inches tall, she sneaked in and out of courtyards in the neighborhood, including those along the rue des Martyrs, to sing to the residents. Seduced by her voice—and her gumption—they threw coins to her from their windows, first wrapping the coins in paper so they would not roll away. I already knew the story's end. Eventually she made it big—as Édith Piaf.

WEDDING
THE
CROWD

· · ·

An American writer who had come to visit France . . .
asked quite naturally what it was that had kept me
here so long. . . It was useless to answer him in words.
I suggested instead that we take a stroll through
the streets.

—HENRY MILLER ON
LIVING IN PARIS

*T*HE RUE DES MARTYRS BECAME AN ADDICTION. I GOT
hooked on its spirit: the rhythm, the collective pleasures, the
bonding with merchants, the way I felt when I walked up and
down it. I became like Louis-Sébastien Mercier, the eighteenth-
century writer and first street reporter of Paris. He wandered on
foot, recording the everyday habits and customs of people of all
classes and professions: prostitutes and policemen, servants and
street vendors, criminals and priests. And artists, beggars, philosophers, greengrocers, and washerwomen. Mercier was driven
by curiosity, not destination. He turned his impressions into

Tableau de Paris, a twelve-volume, twenty-eight-hundred-page collection of sketches of Paris life on the eve of the 1789 Revolution. Alas, Mercier got the revolutionary spirit all wrong—he predicted that Parisians were too self-satisfied to embrace a serious uprising.

"The Parisian's instinct seems to have taught him that the little more liberty he might obtain is not worth fighting for," he wrote. "Any such struggle would imply long effort and stern thinking. He has a short memory for trouble, chalks up no score of his miseries, and has confidence enough in his own strength not to dread too absolute a despotism." *Tableau de Paris* was quickly overtaken by events. Today it is a forgotten jewel of French literature.

I have a complicated relationship with Mercier, as he was the subject of a doctoral dissertation I long ago started and failed to finish. But I have faithfully admired him as a pioneer of walking, wandering, and watching. "I have run around so much while drawing my *Tableau de Paris* that I may be said to have drawn it with my legs," he wrote.

Mercier was more than a detached observer. He flouted social conventions and opened conversations with all sorts of people. "I have made myself acquainted with every class of citizen. . . . Many of the inhabitants of Paris are strangers to their own town. Perhaps this book may teach them something or at least may put before them a clearer and more precise point of view." Immediacy, not deep analysis, was his objective: "My *Tableau* is fresh from my pen, as my eyes and my ears have been able to piece it together."

More than half a century later, the poet Baudelaire—who spent considerable time on the rue des Martyrs—gave new definition to the passionate wanderer-spectator, who by then had become a familiar Parisian type. He called him (it was always a man) a *flâneur*. "The crowd is his habitat, as air is for the bird or water for the fish," he wrote. "His passion and his profession is to wed the crowd. . . . To be away from home, but to feel oneself everywhere at home." As a female *flâneuse*, I had to recalibrate the way I gathered information. I had to wander up and down the street at random hours of the day and night. I had to hang around people and drop in and out of their shops and their lives with regularity. I had to spend long stretches doing nothing. I had to stop looking at my watch. I had to "wed the crowd."

ASIDE FROM THE THEATER, journalism is one of the few professions in which you can play-act. Over the years, I have walked through cornfields in Kansas dressed like a farmer to hear about the worst drought in memory. I've cast myself as a war correspondent in flak jacket and helmet, taking cover from an Iranian air attack in the southern marshes of Iraq. I've played diplomatic analyst wearing a well-cut suit, Chanel pumps, and knitted brow to interview the French president about world peace.

When I lived near the rue du Bac, in the Seventh Arrondissement, I assumed the role of a person of standing: Paris bureau chief for the *New York Times,* married to an American lawyer at one of the most respected French law firms. The streets in the Seventh ooze elitism, not *égalité*. Pedigree, impeccable manners, and—in a perfect world—a country house and hidden wealth add to one's cachet. People didn't think to ask about my Sicilian roots.

On the rue des Martyrs, there is no need to play-act. My family history gives me status. I tell people *"Je suis issue de l'immigration"*—"I have an immigrant background"—and a classic American success story. My grandparents left Sicily for the United States and worked hard to escape poverty. My most treasured family photo shows my grandfather as a young boy in Caltanissetta posing with his white-bearded grandfather, who holds a staff by his side. The photo is about 130 years old. This is the identity I bring to the rue des Martyrs.

I learned the street's early morning rhythm by jogging from bottom to top. The first sound is a six a.m. rush of water, as street sweepers dressed in chartreuse and emerald-green uniforms open valves to send the flow downhill along the gutters. It is part of the Paris cleaning ritual but also a waste of water and a contributing factor to the wet underbelly of Notre-Dame-de-Lorette Church, at the bottom of the street. Depending on the day, I might have to dodge an all-night crowd gathered at Bistrot 82 for more booze and an early breakfast.

By six-thirty, the first food merchants have arrived. The metal shutters of the shops open with a crashing and screeching that ricochets off the old concrete and stone walls. By seven, the roar of trucks delivering food takes over. Every fifteen minutes or so, the 67 bus climbs the street, announcing its presence with a bell. Dogs are late sleepers in my neighborhood, seldom out before eight or eight-thirty. Their masters seem to be a civic-minded bunch who rarely leave behind dog excrement—unlike residents on my old street in a much fancier part of Paris.

The three bells of Notre-Dame-de-Lorette ring at nine a.m., as they will every hour until eight p.m., plus three times a day for the Angelus prayer. Boutiques begin to open at ten a.m. When school lets out, in late afternoon, children crowd the sidewalks with their parents (mostly mothers) or nannies.

A few hours later, the shops shut down just as the cafés and bars fill up. By nine p.m., the restaurants are jammed. The transvestite Cabaret Michou show ends at one a.m.; Bistrot 82 closes an hour or so later—only to open again at five on some mornings. The café-bar-bistro La Fourmi stays open until four a.m. on weekends.

On Sunday mornings, the rue des Martyrs closes to traffic. Sunday Mass is not the main event, since this has been a street of the political left, where church attendance occurs mostly on religious holidays like Christmas and Easter. Instead, people walk up and down, greeting each other with double-cheeked air kisses. Most want to buy the ingredients for Sunday lunch; some want to see and be seen.

But it's not a Paris version of "The Saturday Route," Tom Wolfe's essay about Madison Avenue on Saturday afternoons in the 1960s, when famous people strode briskly and exchanged wet smacks on the cheek. The rue des Martyrs is not as frenzied. People tend to *flâner*, to stroll, dipping in and out of food shops and standing in line patiently when they must. The lines are tolerated, even welcome, since they afford patrons an excuse to chat.

The Sunday morning ritual is familiar to anyone who knows the street. The butcher on the east side sets up a separate counter offering rotisserie chicken and roasted potatoes to satisfy a line of customers who want ready-made food for lunch.

The Levins, who run the bakery a few doors away, add an extra table for baguettes and brioches only, which speeds transactions. Every Sunday, Philippe Levin bakes a brioche loaf with a double dose of butter and a top layer of caramelized sugar. There is a more famous baker up the street, Arnaud Delmontel, who won awards from the Professional Chamber of Artisanal

Bakers and Pastry Chefs for best traditional baguette in 2007 and for best *millefeuille* pastry in 2010. But if an award were given to the best sugar-topped brioche, Philippe would win, hands down.

On the street itself, everyone has a place. Political activists lay claim to the base in front of the barricades that close it off to traffic—a prime spot, since four other streets feed into the rue des Martyrs. On any given Sunday, three or more political parties might compete for the crowd's attention.

The French Communist Party (PCF)—with its Ninth Arrondissement chapter a few blocks away—is particularly active. One Sunday in early 2014, its members distributed a petition condemning an initiative to allow stores to open on Sundays. It accused the "financial powers" of seeking to control the free time of the working class, of damaging small shopkeepers unable to compete with large chains, and of destroying the fabric of society. It asked for new members, using the following pledge: "To make the human choice, to combat the right, to continue the Left Front, I am joining the Communist Party."

LIFE ON THE RUE DES MARTYRS is governed by more than the time of the day and the day of the week. As I wander the street with my notebook, Louis-Sébastien Mercier–style, I am also both bombarded and embraced by the shock of the new.

A designer olive oil shop replaced a greengrocer in 2008; a designer jam shop replaced a clothing store in 2011. A traditional charcuterie had been at No. 6 since 1849; when it moved out, in 2011, a designer rotisserie moved in.

In what seemed like record time, an all-purpose family-run convenience store that stayed open until midnight was replaced by a Subway sandwich shop, then by an Italian food boutique, and finally by a shop offering honey and other bee-related products. Five chocolate shops compete within three blocks.

Farther up the street, a shop selling minimalist modern tableware replaced Et Puis C'est Tout, which specialized in mid-century decorative objects. This was where I used to find vintage Ricard water carafes and 1960s lighted glass geographic world globes cast off by French high schools when the Soviet Union broke up and suddenly there were fifteen republics to paint in. Where once there were stores selling a surprising variety of useful objects, like fabrics and thread, now there are boutiques selling one frivolity at a time: *choux* pastries, madeleines, cookies, Spanish *pata negra* cured ham, and ice creams in New Age flavors like chocolate with *espelette* pepper. In 2014 the London *Sunday Times Magazine* named the rue des Martyrs one of the best shopping streets in the world, signaling its discovery well beyond the neighborhood. The southern part of Pigalle, to its west, has been nicknamed SoPi (pronounced "soapy").

Lamenting change is nothing new. "The sense of neighborhood has gone, never to return," the American art critic John Russell wailed in his classic 1975 study of Paris. "The one-person shop, the solitary craftsman, the frugal, secret, and yet dignified life—all have been lost." Eight years later, in an essay called "My Paris," the novelist Saul Bellow sounded a similar death knell: "A certain decrepit loveliness is giving way to unattractive, overpriced, overdecorated newness."

The saddest physical and cultural loss on the rue des Martyrs occurred in the early 1970s, when developers razed the nineteenth-century circus complex at the boundary of the Ninth and Eighteenth Arrondissements. Named Cirque Fernando and then

Cirque Medrano, it was housed in a grand sixteen-sided structure and became a showpiece for some of the world's most gifted clowns. Poets and painters drew inspiration from it. Edgar Degas painted *Miss La La at the Cirque Fernando,* which depicted an aerialist hanging from a rope by her teeth. One of Georges Seurat's most famous works, *The Circus,* has at its focal point a young woman in a yellow tutu balanced on one foot atop a galloping white horse. Renoir painted acrobats and female jugglers from here, Toulouse-Lautrec a rider on horseback. Buster Keaton, the American actor, comedian, vaudevillian, and stunt performer, and his wife, Eleanor, performed at the Cirque Medrano for several years after World War II. Until the circus closed, the roar of lions filled the street, and when the wind blew, the smell of hay and animal dung permeated shops, homes, and schools.

As television grew more popular in the 1960s, the lure of the circus faded. For a while the structure survived as an auditorium for beer festivals and theatrical productions. In 1972, it was torn down. "So much sadness in these ruins—a bit of Paris has died, has left us, taking forever one of Montmartre's many charms," a television newscaster announced in somber tones, as black-and-white footage showed the wreckage at the site. An eight-story concrete horror of apartments atop a Carrefour supermarket replaced it.

One day my husband spotted a "For Sale" sign on the top floor. "Hey, there's an apartment for sale!" he exclaimed. "Isn't this a prime example of the Brutalist school?"

I had never heard of the Brutalist school, although the building certainly fits the name. Andy said Brutalist buildings were fashionable in the mid-twentieth century. They often mixed family housing and shopping centers and looked like concrete fortresses.

He got that right.

"We could have a great view of Montmartre," he said.

"Sure," I replied. "And live in the ugliest building in Paris."

NOT ALL HAS BEEN LOST on the rue des Martyrs—not yet.

Maybe it's because progress has come slowly to this part of Paris. Annick Poulain, a young professional who lives with her husband and son at No. 23—in an apartment her grandparents bought in 1914—told me her grandmother lived without a refrigerator until 1970. She never had the luxury of a bathtub or a shower but washed herself in a basin in an alcove off the kitchen until she died, in 1974.

Maybe it's because, until recent years, the street was neither elegant nor trendy. From his childhood, Thierry Cazaux remembers two butchers who sold nothing but horse meat and two others who sold only organ meats, like kidneys and tripe. Streetwalkers outnumbered children. Thierry met his first prostitute as a schoolboy; she took up her post every morning on the rue des Martyrs outside the gate of the Cité Malesherbes, where he lived. "It was her spot, her territory," he said. "We always said hello to each other as I went to school, and she called me by my name. I don't know how old I was when I realized what she was doing there."

Maybe it's because new isn't always bad—and is, occasionally, quite wonderful. The *pata negra* at the Spanish ham shop is, well, as close as you get to a gastronomic orgasm, and it did push a second-rate men's clothing store out of business. (The old-time food merchants agree that any initiative for the sake of gastronomy, however chichi, is all for the good.) The salted caramels at

the Henri Le Roux chocolate shop transport those who try them
to the sea off the coast of Brittany. And the olive oil shop? One of
the best Mother's Day presents I ever received was a selection of
six varieties of olive oil in sweet little tins, each with its own spout.

The street has been adapting, fighting, and succumbing to
change for more than a century. It wins one and loses one. The
net result is that something essential remains unchanged. The
rue des Martyrs has been spared much of the chainstorification
that has culturally homogenized other Paris streets as rents have
soared, artisanal work has been devalued, and the city has
become more prosperous. There are few tourists, except around
the Abbesses Métro station, the closest stop to Sacré-Coeur. Yes,
we have Antoine & Lili, Les Petites, and Maje—three small,
classy, ready-to-wear fashion chains—but no Zara, H&M, Star-
bucks, or Sephora.

For every threat of a chain store, there is a new artisanal merchant. For every building that disappears, there's the discovery
of a marvel once thought lost.

A hardware store has been at No. 1 since 1865.

The café–bistro–wine bar has been a café at No. 2 for more
than a century.

A butcher shop at No. 3 has been run by the same family
since 1899.

A pharmacy at No. 4 appears in Paris archives as early as 1848.

No. 10 has been a bakery since 1868; No. 48, a cheese store
since 1915.

Often one food shop replaces another selling the same item.
The Delmontel bakery, at No. 39, for example, is in an Art Nouveau building that has housed a bakery since 1902.

The law is on the side of continuity on the rue des Martyrs.

Paris passed the Local Urbanism Plan law in 2006 to improve the quality of life, reduce income inequality, and preserve the city's architectural heritage. It gives zoning protection to more than sixty streets, including this one.

Ground-floor artisanal shops producing or selling food or crafts can be replaced only by other artisanal shops. No big chain or clothing stores are allowed. The bottom of the rue des Martyrs (up to the rue Victor-Massé) enjoys this designation, as do the nearby rue Cadet and rue Richer; the rue Mouffetard, in the Latin Quarter; the rue Montorgueil, on the Right Bank; and the rue Cler, not far from the Eiffel Tower.

The law prevented Monoprix, a major chain that sells food, clothing, and cosmetics, from taking over a decades-old pastry shop on the rue des Martyrs. Monoprix paid about 700,000 euros for the space, with the intention of opening a beauty emporium, and pledged to install a manicure service to give it artisan status. At that point, Jacques Bravo, then the neighborhood mayor, intervened. He broke the Monoprix deal and persuaded Sébastien Gaudard, one of the fanciest (but one of the best) pastry chefs in Paris, to move into the shop. Gaudard makes all of his pastries, breads, ice creams, and chocolates on-site.

Bravo was widely respected for his accomplishments as mayor of the Ninth from 2001 to the spring of 2014. But the Socialists' era ended when Bravo's deputy mayor, Pauline Véron, lost the mayoral election to the center-right candidate by 159 votes, less than 1 percent. Younger, conservative voters, it seems, care more about wealth accumulation than Socialist projects like low-income housing and free home health care for the elderly.

Of all the recent changes in the neighborhood, this political one may prove to be the most far-reaching.

NOW, *THIS*
IS BUTTER!

...

I've noticed that people who know
how to eat are rarely idiots.

—GUILLAUME APOLLINAIRE,
Le flâneur des deux rives

*T*HE RUE DES MARTYRS HAS ALWAYS BEEN ABOUT COMMERCE, especially the sale of food. I am inordinately passionate about food. This feeling has a lot to do with my father, who taught me the importance of eating well long before I moved to France. From the time I was five years old, he owned a store selling Italian specialties to working-class Italian-Americans in Niagara Falls, New York. I take his spirit with me every time I step out onto the rue des Martyrs.

Tony Sciolino was honest, faithful to my mother, and a good provider. I admired his commitment to paying bills in full on time. "You're only as good as your good name!" he'd say, an expression he had learned from his father. But he was not an easy man.

He demanded obedience at home and the highest grades at school. My strongest childhood memory of his affection is from when I was about seven; he carried me from the car to the house after I had been to the hospital. His idea of an ideal Sunday outing was to pile my sister, my brother, and me into the car for a long ride and tune the radio to a Yankees game. There was little room for conversation. To this day, I cannot hear a radio broadcast of a baseball game without getting a headache.

My father was the first-born and only son of Sicilian immigrants. He beat the odds and graduated from college during the Depression. During World War II, he was drafted into the army and was assigned for a while to work as a mechanic in an airplane-engine factory in Buffalo, a cushy job that allowed him to go home every night to his mother's cooking and his own bed. Eventually the Army Air Corps shipped him to Italy and Morocco, as a sergeant. He never saw action, but he managed to sneak in a visit to Sicily to meet some long-lost relatives. He gave them cigarettes and chocolates. They fed him well.

After the war, my father worked as a tax inspector for the IRS, married, and moved with my mother into an upstairs flat in his parents' house. Every evening, he filled a bottle from one of two oak barrels in the basement that held the wine he and my grandfather made in the backyard every summer. He read Buffalo's evening newspaper, ate the meal my mother cooked from scratch, and drank his wine.

On a commercial street several blocks away, my mother's brothers ran Columbia Market, an Italian food store so big and prosperous that it served as the neighborhood supermarket. They proposed that my father open a branch store twenty miles away, in Niagara Falls. In 1954, he became the owner and manager of the new store, but after a falling out with his brothers-in-law a few years later, he struck out on his own. He changed the store's name to Latina Importing Company, did his own product selection and buying, and eliminated the middlemen. The brothers opened a new Columbia Market a few blocks away. They and my father never spoke again.

My father's "office" was a shellacked piece of pine balanced on two empty olive barrels under the stairs. A two-hundred-pound provolone cheese sat on one of the store's counters. For years, he used his 1957 Plymouth station wagon as both family car and delivery truck, and he loaded it every morning with still-warm Italian bread from a bakery near our house. He sold two varieties: a quick-rise loaf for seventeen cents, and one made with sourdough leavening for nineteen cents. When I lived at home while going to college, I delivered the bread early on Saturday mornings. I also managed his correspondence, paid his bills, and worked at the cash register. He paid me ten dollars a day. The job was not optional.

My father communicated with many of his customers in a rough Sicilian dialect and taught me the art of delivering small pleasures through food and conversation. No matter how cold the winter, how deep the snow, how bad the economy, how serious the problem, he believed anyone could find comfort in a family meal, even one as simple as penne with bacon, onions, and a can of Progresso cannellini beans. "Everybody has to eat!" he would say.

Because most of his customers were working-class, he had to keep prices low. He sold dried beans, grains, and spices in open bins, not because it was fashionable but because he could provide better value and better quality without industrial packaging. He sold macaroni—it wasn't called "pasta" in those days—in ten-pound bags. He showed customers how a macaroni-making machine could do double duty as a paper shredder.

He never bought retail. "Chisel them down!" he told me and my siblings as he taught us how to pay less. He bartered with merchants at the open-air market next door: Italian cheeses, salami, olive oil, amaretto cookies, and other delicacies in exchange for fresh produce, strip steaks, even lobsters. At Christmas, his two female employees assembled gift baskets overflowing with candied fruits, nuts, panettone, and pastries for delivery to people who had done him favors.

In 1991, a local merchant group honored him for his "entrepreneurship." Another year, he won a Caribbean cruise for being the number one wholesale distributor of a brand of hot sauce. Once, when he installed a new window in our house, he left behind his signature in black marker on the aluminum frame: "Tony the Food King."

I didn't appreciate my father much during his lifetime. He believed the world was a dangerous place, that only family could be trusted, and even then not always. More than a decade after his death, bonding with food merchants on the rue des Martyrs has become my way of connecting with him.

SOME MORNINGS, I SIT AT A SMALL, Formica-topped sidewalk table at Le Dream Café, at No. 8. It used to be Café le Commerce, a down-at-the-heels kind of place where a big-screen television was always on, tuned to an all-sports channel, and the regulars stood at the long zinc bar for a morning beer or a glass of house wine, an old workers' custom. It did so well that the owners closed it down for renovations one day and opened a few months later as Le Dream Café, a café–wine bar–restaurant.

One wall was lined with bottles of wine, another with pale new stone made to look old.

Happily, it retains its down-to-earth spirit. The television stayed, as did a poster-sized blow-up of a one-hundred-year-old black-and-white postcard of the rue des Martyrs. The café opens at six-thirty a.m. to welcome the early working crowd. The butchers from across the street arrive holding half baguettes with ham for their first break, at ten. If Sébastien Dominique, my favorite butcher, is with them, he'll chew and swallow, wipe his mouth clean, and kiss me on both cheeks.

Yves Chataigner, the cheesemonger across the street, comes for four espressos (two each for him and his wife, Annick), which he carries on a tray to his shop. One morning he kissed my hand—correctly; lips did not touch skin. I told him he was much more refined than former president Jacques Chirac, who always smacked the woman's hand with his lips. At that, he clasped my hand and rubbed his thumb on it, just the slightest flirtation from a guy in his eighties.

"You know what they used to say about Chirac?" he asked.

"Five minutes, shower included!" I replied, proud to be in the know. That was Chirac's nickname, because he was such an efficient ladies' man, once upon a time.

Yves told me a new one: "They called him the machine gun!"

Momo Allili, the morning manager, serves the best *café crème* on the street (his hot chocolate is even better), in heavy porcelain cups and saucers stamped "Cafés Richard." The croissants and baguettes are made early in the morning at the Levin family bakery next door.

One morning I did a taste test of three varieties of butter sold at the Chataigners' cheese shop. I sat at my regular table and sliced a baguette. The sweet butter from Normandy was rich but too unctuous; the sweet butter from Charentes, firmer and drier; the salted butter, also from Charentes, much saltier than store-bought.

"You want *the* best butter in the world?" Momo asked. "Just wait."

He disappeared into the back room. "Now, *this* is butter," he said, emerging with a saucer piled high with a deep yellow substance. He said his butter is made with unpasteurized milk from the Kabylie region of Algeria, where he was born and where much of his family still lives. His younger brother Mahmoud, who owns the café, makes the butter himself and smuggles it into France. Momo says it is too special to serve to customers. (Doing so would certainly violate European Union food standards.)

The butter was textured and dry, with a pungent taste of ripe cheese. I don't know if it was the best butter in the world, but I didn't care. What mattered was that Momo had shared his precious stash with me.

Late one morning, when Sébastien the butcher offered to buy me a *café crème*, Momo brought it with a swirl of cream and chocolate and chocolate sprinkles on top. "Made with love," Momo said.

Sébastien is the most outgoing butcher at the Boucherie Roger Billebault, part of a small chain that has been owned by the Billebault family since 1899. He starts work at six a.m. He was planning a three-week vacation to a small chalet somewhere in the south, he told me. There would be water sports and other activities for his two daughters, ages fourteen and ten, who live with their mother.

"Do you want to get married again?" I asked.

"I do, but how to find a wife?" he said. "With my work schedule, who's going to put up with that? Oh, I've had a few adventures, don't get me wrong. But nothing serious. And I won't introduce my daughters to anyone who isn't 'the one.'"

"Excuse me, could you help me?" asked a woman at the next table, extending her right arm. "The string on my bracelet is loose. Could you tighten it for me?"

She was forty or so. She wore a fitted T-shirt, capri pants, gym shoes, and no makeup. How long had she been sitting there? Had she been listening to our conversation?

Sébastien lifted her wrist and examined the knot on the bracelet. He pulled the string, and the bracelet tightened.

"That wasn't so hard," said Sébastien. They exchanged smiles.

The woman's name was Laurence. She lived in the Fourteenth Arrondissement (not far from Sébastien!) in the south of Paris. She was unmarried and had no children. For twenty years she had had an office job, but three years ago she had quit.

"What do you do now?" I asked.

"Je suis une KHAT-seet-air," she said.

"A what?"

"Une KHAT-seet-air."

"Of course," I said. "A cat-sitter."

Laurence had joined a friend's dog-walking business to handle the cat side of things. Summer is the season for cats. The French tend to take their dogs but not their cats on vacation. As everyone knows, cats are homebodies and want to be left behind. But in ninety-degree weather, with no air-conditioning, Paris cats need Laurence.

"I make less money than I did before, but my life is so much better," she said.

She gave Sébastien and me business cards showing a big-eyed dog with a smile. "A Dog in the City. Individualized dog-walking," it read.

"We haven't printed cat cards yet," she explained.

"I like cats," said Sébastien.

As we said our good-byes, I whispered to Laurence, "He's a wonderful guy. He's looking for a wife."

I followed Sébastien back to the butcher shop. "You see, Sébastien, it's not that hard."

I SOMETIMES WRITE about food for the *New York Times*, and occasionally share my discoveries with the neighbors. When I wrote about American Thanksgiving one year, I brought samples of cornbread-apple stuffing to my favorite bakers. At Christmas, when I wrote about chocolate, I brought back dozens of bars from Bonnat, a small chocolate maker near Grenoble, and passed them out like Santa.

One spring I harvested white asparagus. A cold, wet winter in France meant the special white variety had come late to the rue des Martyrs. It was expensive, at ten euros a pound, and because it had been trucked a long way, it was dull and wrinkled.

So I set out to harvest my own, in the deepest part of the Landes, near the Spanish border. When I returned to Paris with two shopping bags of white asparagus, I gave some to my greengrocer friend Ezzidine.

"I'll cook them for my wife!" he exclaimed. But Ezzidine is a fruit and vegetable guy, not a chef. He overcooked them, and they turned limp and stringy.

"They tasted great!" he said. I didn't believe him.

Shortly after New Year's, I saw that he had four baskets of fresh cranberries on the display. "What are you doing with fresh cranberries?" I asked. "Thanksgiving was in November."

Ezzidine said he'd ordered them for his French customers, thinking that in an era of culinary globalization, they might want cranberry sauce with their Christmas turkeys. But the French are not particularly inventive about holiday cooking. No one bought them.

He told me that if I took all of them, he'd shave a third off the price.

I said I would, and he produced four more baskets. He must have felt guilty about foisting so many cranberries on me, so he said, "Ah, I haven't given you your New Year's present." He handed me a long, slim bottle of olive oil, produced not far from his home on the Tunisian island of Djerba.

I made a vat of cranberry sauce with orange rind and just enough sugar to cut the bite, like my mother used to do. I gave a jar to Ezzidine. "I could charge a lot for this, but never you!" I said. "Enjoy!"

Another day, baskets of strange oval shapes with velvety skin the color of celadon turned up: fresh almonds. Ezzidine slammed a nut against a wooden pillar to crack the tough skin and fleshy covering. He removed them to reveal an almond kernel. When I put it to my mouth, he stopped me.

"You have to peel it now," he said. He pinched the skin with a fingernail and pulled it back. He did it again and again until he had a smooth, white almond. "Now you can eat it."

It tasted like almond, only crunchy and fresh like a water chestnut.

"But it's so much work," I said.

"It's not the eating that counts," he said. "It's the process of cracking and peeling. After dinner, with a glass of mint tea, in front of the television, with all the family together. There is nothing better."

Over time, Ezzidine began to share his stories: about his niece's wedding in Djerba and his fantasy of one day kissing Sharon Stone.

"You know what I love about her?" he said. "She's so natural. She's never had any work done."

"What, are you kidding me? Of course she has," I said.

"Well, maybe just a little filler, but no cutting," he said.

How in the world had he come to this conclusion, I can't begin to guess.

He showed me photos of his wife and their nine-year-old daughter. He confessed that he was sad on his day off, when his wife was at work and he was home alone. "I wish I had my customers," he said. He sounded like my father.

Since the rue des Martyrs is about food, it must be about wine, too. The butcher and cheese shops and one of the fish shops sell wine. So do the take-out *traiteurs,* the smoked salmon shop, the Spanish *pata negra* ham shop, the beer emporium, and the convenience store with no name. The two supermarkets sell wine so respectable that some of their labels are featured in wine reviews. Terra Corsa, the Corsican *traiteur,* sells a large selection of Corsican wines. Pelops, the Greek *traiteur,* sells a small selection of Greek wines. Chez Plume, a high-end take-out place with a small eat-in space in the back, offers an ambitious range of "natural" French wines (made pesticide- and additive-free, with minimum sulfur) starting at 6.50 euros to accompany all kinds of free-range fowl: chickens from the Landes, ducks, guinea hens, quails, and pigeons.

The rue des Martyrs boasts four wine shops. Nicolas, the outlet of a nationwide chain, sells a wide variety of passable, well-priced wines. Nysa, which opened in 2014, is one of ten outlets in Paris whose mission, the company says, is to bring "democracy" and New Age thinking about wine to the table. Emotional connection and pairings with specific foods are more important than vintages here. So there are special wines for "a big day," "between girlfriends," and "love at first sight."

I am a light drinker and, therefore, a mediocre student of wine. I'm not good at playing the field by trying a lot of wines, year after year, which I'm told is the only way to master the wine universe. I can't tell the difference between a Côte de Beaune and a Côte de Nuits. Not even *French Wine for Dummies* makes me smarter. So I need help.

My close-to-home, go-to place is Le Repaire de Bacchus, an outlet of a small Paris-area chain with good wines and sound advice. Its merchants woo customers with regional promotions, and they never make me feel stupid. The day the shop mounted a celebration of Italian wines, it won me over with its selection of proseccos. Since then, we talk about Italy and I don't always have to buy French.

At the top of the rue des Martyrs, Sébastien Guénard is a wine pioneer. A thirty-something chef, he is the owner of the bistro Miroir, the only quality bistro on the Montmartre end of the street. When Mario, the butcher across the street from Miroir, retired after twenty-five years, Sébastien bought him out, and in 2009 he opened Cave du Miroir, a retail wine store and wine bar

that specializes in natural wines from small, little-known vine-
yards. He built shelves up to the thirteen-foot ceiling and filled
them with wines, focusing on varieties he knew from visiting his
grandfather's home in the village of Soings-en-Sologne in central France. His favorite is a 2012 Racines, an obscure red wine
produced by Claude Courtois and made with several varieties of
grapes from that area; it sells for seventeen euros. He installed a
simple counter that does double duty as the bar; added a few
stools, tables, and chairs; and retained the bare, cracked concrete
floor. "My goal is to have the best of the best for as little money as
possible," he said. "I want my clients to feel good because they
haven't been robbed."

His customers prefer sipping to guzzling, even on the nights
when the Cave is open until midnight. His neighbors continually
express gratitude that Mario the butcher's departure didn't bring
still another clothing boutique to the street.

Even when wholesale prices of fine old vintages soared,
Sébastien didn't raise prices, either at the bistro or at the wine bar.
A 1989 Saint-Émilion, which he called one of the finest wines of
our day, is listed on the bistro menu at more than 500 euros. "I
want to be accessible, unpretentious," he said. "I want people to
come in and know they are getting a deal. Not that five hundred
euros is nothing. But it's a gift."

"A gift?" I asked. "Five hundred euros is a gift? A round-trip
ticket to New York in low season isn't much more!"

"It's more than triple that price at a three-star restaurant
across town," he said. "So yes, if you want to experience this
wine, it's a gift."

Then he came back down to earth.

"If it hasn't gone bad, that is! And if it has, then it really will be a gift. Zero."

GIVEN MY FAMILY HISTORY, I know a lot more about cheese than wine, and more about Italian than French cheese. As Yves and Annick Chataigner, the couple who have run the cheese shop for half a century, enlightened me, we formed a special bond. Yves is in his eighties, Annick about seventy. They have been married for more than fifty years. In a country where the thirty-five-hour week is the law for the salaried employees, they work close to sixty hours, over six days.

In the old days, merchants on the street tended to live in modest apartments above their shops. The Chataigners are among the few who still do. Annick became a mother at eighteen. Their grandchildren are already in their twenties. Without day-to-day family responsibilities, they play as hard as they work. Yves has a weekly tennis game. Annick goes to the Club Med gym down the street four times a week. Every winter they take long vacations to warm, exotic places like the Dominican Republic and Mauritius.

They keep the business that bears their name, at No. 3 rue des Martyrs, simple. They do not use a cash register or even a calculator. They add up purchases by hand on tiny slips of paper.

Yves is not happy about the tourists who visit his shop. He talked of his frustrations with foreigners who don't know the rules.

"They come in here and they don't say *bonjour,*" he said. "The Italians are the worst. They touch the cheese with their fingers! One Italian guy who came in insisted, because he said that in

Italy you have the right to touch the cheese. We need to educate them in our ways."

I said, "Do you know that in the United States you don't usually say hello when you enter a shop? It might be considered an interruption of workers doing their job."

"Ah, bon?" Yves asked. *Oh, really?* He couldn't believe it.

I told him I wanted to learn about French cheese.

"If you want to get serious, you have to go to school," he said. "I spent three years in a cheese school. You can't just spend an hour or two."

"Well, I have to start somewhere."

I made an appointment for a private cheese lesson the following week. When I arrived, accompanied by a young researcher, Marie Missioux, Yves was ready. He said he had been brushing up on cheese factoids from a guide he had found in a closet.

"How many kilos of milk do you need to make a kilo of Parmesan?" he asked.

"Three?" guessed Marie.

"More!" said Yves.

"Ten?" I asked.

"More!"

"Fifteen?"

"Right, just like a Comté!"

He said that *l'affinage*—the ripening process—requires three constants: humidity, a temperature of eight degrees Celsius (about forty-six degrees Fahrenheit), and good ventilation. He explained the four categories of cow-milk cheeses: *pâte dure*, or hard cheeses, like Comté, Beaufort, and Gruyère; *pâte fleurie*, or soft-ripened cheeses, like Camembert and Brie; *pâte persillée*, or blue-veined cheeses shot with penicillin spores, like bleu d'Auvergne, and *pâte lavée,* or washed-rind cheeses, like Maroilles and Munster.

Roquefort, the "cheese of kings and popes," is made with sheep's milk, he said.

"I once spent a day with Jacques Carles, who makes the best Roquefort in France," I said.

"Not a night, too?" Yves asked. "There's a song that goes like that," and he started singing, "A day, a night . . ."

He said we'd begin with Camembert. He took a round from the shelf and removed its white plastic wrapping. "First, there is how the Camembert looks," he said. "The cheese must have aged. When there is white in the middle like this one, it is too young.

"Then there is the feel; you have to make contact with the Camembert. I first squeeze the sides of its outer crust. Then there is the way your thumb feels when you press on the center. There can be no resistance. Resistance means the Camembert has no heart. For the Camembert to have a heart, your thumb has to feel softness. There must be a *partage.*"

That word pops up so often in just about any conversation about food: *partage.* It signals that you're not alone, especially when you're communing with Camembert as if it were a living thing. Yves pulled a bright white Camembert from another shelf. When he pushed on it, the cheese pushed back. He said it needed fifteen more days. Now I got it—making physical contact with a Camembert is essential, but only he could do it.

"After this lesson, Elaine will not need us to choose her cheese," said Annick.

"So how long will it take to become a Camembert expert?" I asked.

"To be really at ease with a Camembert—maybe a year and a

half, and even then, our clients might not want to be served by a newcomer," said Yves. Apparently, the hierarchy of cheese was once so rigid that only the highest-ranking cheesemonger could serve the finest cheeses, followed by the lower-level cheesemonger, who served bargain cheeses outdoors, followed by the egg lady, who was allowed to sell eggs but not cheese.

"Even now, some customers will only be served by Yves, not me!" said Annick.

Yves wanted to end our lesson and do his bookkeeping. But I realized I knew little about his background. I began to probe.

"We lived in the country," he said. "My parents had a great deal of misfortune. My father was a carpenter. He started his own business, and borrowed money. In the end he couldn't pay his debts, and everything was taken away. He was a beaten man. He went to work in a granite quarry. But working in a quarry, it is an alien place. You drink to survive, but it makes things worse.

"Back then, we used to say, 'When there is no money in the wallet, there is the devil in the house.' We lived in a hole, in the middle of nowhere. Everyone was miserable."

Yves was the eighth of nine children; his father died of tuberculosis soon after the last child was born. Yves said he became sick with tuberculosis as well and spent two years in a sanatorium.

I wanted to know more, but Yves fell silent.

Annick stepped in. "You're going to make him cry, Elaine." She gave her husband an order: "Go, talk about cheese. Go!" she said.

Yves turned away and stared down at a shelf of Camembert rounds. He couldn't stop his tears. The French aren't huggers, but I couldn't help myself. I hugged him.

"Americans do this," I said. "It's a gesture of friendship."

Yves managed to go on. He described a life of hardship, of having to leave home at thirteen to work as a field hand. He had no more formal schooling and slept in an unheated barn with the cows. But he learned accounting during his military service, then apprenticed in a cheese shop, and eventually got a job as assistant to a cheesemonger on the rue des Martyrs.

When it came time for the boss to retire, he lent Yves money to buy the shop.

"I became like his son," he said. "Everyone knew it."

Yves did not want to end with gushy sentiment. So he selected a smelly yellowish-brown cheese, a six-month-old Corsican *brebis*. "Attack it!" he said. "It's the strongest cheese in the shop. After a taste of this, a glass of red goes down very well. I love to eat it—but only once a year!"

It smelled like socks that had been worn for three days, then left in a damp clothes hamper to ripen even more.

"Ha! You'll remember this cheese lesson," said Yves.

He was right. The taste of *brebis* lingered for days.

TO CATCH A MOUSE

...

"You're right, Dad. Who am I kidding?
We are what we are, and we're rats."

——REMY, THE FRENCH RODENT,
IN THE ANIMATED FILM *Ratatouille*

"He's not a regular rat, or even a super rat.
He's just a scared little mouse."

——HOLLY GOLIGHTLY IN *Breakfast at Tiffany's*

THE MERCHANTS ON THE RUE DES MARTYRS OFFER
advice about everything. I figured I could get to know them better by discussing my mouse problem.

One August, we returned from vacation to find that a slim,
four-inch-long gray mouse had settled comfortably into our
apartment. It made brief appearances in the evening. First it ran
into the hallway from the storage closet. Then it jumped from a
narrow space under the oven onto the kitchen floor. We last saw
it scurrying diagonally across the dining room.

Andy and I had dealt with a rodent before, when we lived in

New York City. Late one Saturday night, we heard something digging through the garbage in the main room of our Soho loft. When Andy investigated, he came eyeball-to-eyeball with a rat—a very large, fat rat, at least a foot long. They froze, stared each other down, then retreated.

I called a twenty-four-hour extermination service but got a recording. I called around to hotels, but the cheapest room I could find was $200. That seemed like a raw deal since it was already one a.m.

My husband remains calm in a storm, and his inclination was to wait it out until morning. I, however, went into action mode. I called the local fire department. The firefighter on duty thought the story was funny. So I called the police. Andy, sensing that I was out of control, didn't waste time trying to stop me.

"My husband is a homicide prosecutor in Brooklyn, so I like the police," I said.

Two young police officers arrived, guns drawn. They trapped the rat in a big garbage pail (or so we thought), threw away the garbage, and said good night. Andy and I went back to bed. Two hours later, the rat was back. Days would pass before it left us for good.

Until the mouse came calling, I had had only one close sighting of a Paris rodent. And it wasn't even real. One evening in the late 1970s, I was sitting at an outdoor table at the Deux Magots café on the place Saint-Germain-des-Prés. There, on one of the most tourist-trodden corners of Paris, I saw the legendary Rat Man in action. He had a reputation for accosting strangers on the street and flashing a fake rodent. He flashed; the strangers cringed (and sometimes threw money at him to make him go away); the café sitters enjoyed the show. It was said that at one point he used live rats.

This time was different. This was not street theater. Our new rodent was real. I stopped by Pyro Folie's, the fireworks and special effects store on the ground floor below our apartment, to ask the manager if the shop had mice. "No, they don't like the taste of cellulose or explosives," said Marie-Ange Roidor, a woman of about fifty with a smoky Jeanne Moreau voice. "I never see them. But I hear them."

Hear them?

"Sometimes I hear scratching, gnawing, running," she said. She imitated a rodent, biting the air with her teeth and scratching it with curled fingers.

"When was the last time you heard one?" I asked.

"Oh, about three weeks ago."

It turns out that for several years, Paris has been besieged by mice. CS3D, France's official disinfection, de-insectization, de-ratization trade association, estimates that the city is home to six million mice, many of which live well in the city's best restaurants, the Élysée Palace, and the prime minister's residence. At one point, a video allegedly showing mice scurrying around the kitchen and the staff canteen of the Galeries Lafayette department store surfaced on YouTube.

The problem in my neighborhood was especially serious around this time because of ongoing construction work. There were so many mice that late one night one of my neighbors was peering through the lit-up window of a bakery on the rue des Martyrs and spotted two of them frolicking in the flour. The Pyro Folie's manager suggested that I borrow our building's unofficial cat, which belongs to Ilda, the concierge.

So I asked Ilda about her cat, silky black with the lean and hungry look of a killer. "Pompom? My fourteen-year-old Pompom? No use," she said. "He thinks he's a cat of luxury. When he sees a mouse, he just doesn't care."

I called Jean-Pierre, our upstairs neighbor, who has lived in the building forever. I described our mouse. He was impressed by its size. "Hmm, that's a beautiful mouse," he said. "Either a beautiful mouse or a petite rat!"

Calling a mouse beautiful is an example of what the French call *second degré*. *Second degré* requires irony, and at its best makes you seem intelligent, clever, and funny. Jean-Pierre thought he was being funny.

I asked him about Hygiène 75, the extermination shop in the neighborhood. A sign on the window says it specializes in "de-insectization," "de-ratization," and "de-pigeoning." One window display includes a small gray mouse struggling helplessly in a trap while two other mice flee. A variety of poisons, including rat pasta, complete the decor. Estimates are free.

Jean-Pierre warned me off exterminators. He said they would overcharge and fill the apartment with toxic chemicals that wouldn't do the job. He told me to lay down traps: either classic spring-loaded snap types that break a rodent's neck or modern glue versions that "immobilize" but don't immediately kill the beast. The first is quick and messy, the second slow and unnerving.

On the way to the hardware store for more information, I stopped at Guy Lellouche's antiques store. "Put a piece of old Gruyère in a snap trap," he said. He made a chopping motion with his hand. "Tack! The head will come off!"

If that didn't work in two days, he said, try a finer cheese.

I was thinking more of a Maginot Line of steel wool. I had learned this battlefield tactic from the New York exterminator who eventually rid us of our rat. You plug all the holes in your walls with steel wool, and hope that it will be too tough for mice to chew through. So at the hardware store, I loaded up with three grades of steel wool and a variety of traps: snap traps, glue traps, and little plastic "houses" that lure a mouse inside and shut the door after it. The guy in charge of pest-extermination products was dubious about steel wool. "Rodents have no bones," he said. "They're all cartilage; they can crawl through anything."

"Of course they have bones," I said. I had just read a story about the discovery in China of a 160-million-year-old fossil of a super-rodent.

I came back later in the day for more steel wool and proudly announced that I had laid down all the traps.

"You wore gloves, right?" he asked.

"You didn't tell me to wear gloves." I looked down at my hands.

"You always wear gloves," he said. "Rodents are cunning. They can detect the smell of humans. If you didn't wear gloves, your traps are useless."

He told me to start over. And to use chocolate as bait. "Rodents like good chocolate," he said.

"What kind of chocolate?" I asked. I had no idea that French rodents had such fine palates.

"Milk chocolate for mice," he said. "Some even like meat. Butcher shops are full of rats."

I headed to the butcher shop, where they thought my rodent problem was hilarious.

"You're American, so use your gun!" said Sébastien, my favorite butcher. He pretended to shoot a rifle. "Poof! It's dead."

Maybe Sébastien would be my savior. "Are you a hunter? Do you know how to hunt mice?"

"The only thing I hunt is beautiful women," he said.

The butchers got an even bigger laugh out of that. Then they sent me off to talk to the real rodent expert, Yves Chataigner, the cheesemonger two doors down.

When you're in a war over who gets the cheese, it pays to be preemptive. Yves has a regular arrangement with a commercial exterminator. He advised me to put a small piece of aged Comté cheese on the traps. It costs about thirty euros a pound. He cut me a piece to taste and said there was no charge.

Why aged Comté, which is more expensive than young Comté or Gruyère?

"It's got a good, strong rind," he said.

"What's rind got to do with it?"

A female customer jumped into the conversation.

"You have to have a strong rind and jam it in the trap at just the right level," she said. "A smart mouse knows how to grab the cheese before the trap strikes." Then she advised me never to buy ready-made glue traps but to make my own; she launched into a long, detailed explanation of how to construct them. She said that the pungent smell of old kitty litter might be effective—cat urine can be a powerful deterrent—and that barn owls can kill more than a dozen mice a night. I was out of my league. How did this woman, dressed in elegant white, know so much about rodents?

"Ha, ha!" she laughed. "I've had a country house for years! You learn about rodents. You kill the rats, of course. But the mice! They're rather sweet-looking. Just enjoy them."

I should have known that the French would like rodents. A number of the fables of Jean de La Fontaine involve mice or rats, which are often portrayed as kind, curious, and generous rather than dirty, disease-bearing, and disgusting. In "The Lion and the Rat," for example, the rat displays patience and perseverance in saving the life of the King of the Beasts. In "The Cat and an Old Rat," the experienced rat is too clever to be deceived by the cat's tricks. In "The Rat and the Oyster," the country rat "of little brains" shows gumption and curiosity in exploring the world, but his naïveté and innocence land him inside the oyster's grip.

I tried to think of our French mouse as a small version of Remy, the anthropomorphic French rodent in the 2007 film *Ratatouille*. Remy appreciated good food and longed to cook. He was the secret "little chef" for Linguini, a garbage boy at a fancy Paris restaurant. Remy wanted to be a real chef, but he knew he would always be seen as a rat. "I pretend to be a rat for my father; I pretend to be a human through Linguini," Remy says during one poignant moment in the film.

I didn't get the chance to befriend our mouse. In the days that followed, it did not return. Ilda, the concierge, reported a sighting in one of the converted maids' rooms on the sixth floor. Just like Remy in *Ratatouille*, it had good taste. It ate pistachios and a piece of chocolate cake but didn't touch the garbage.

THE MEANING
OF
MARTYRDOM

...

The other day when I was walking I got to thinking.
How do the French name their streets?

—ART BUCHWALD,
AMERICAN HUMOR COLUMNIST

𝒫ARIS HAS MORE THAN SIXTY-TWO HUNDRED STREETS, boulevards, avenues, and passages. Their names fall into several categories: kings (Henri IV, François I), American presidents (Wilson, Roosevelt), military victories (Iéna, Aboukir), important dates (September 4, after the day in 1870 when the Third Republic was created; November 11, after Armistice Day, marking the end of World War I), trades (bakers, drapers), about 175 saints (Jean, Paul, Georges), cities of the world (Tehran, Cairo, Rome), and the eccentric (Street of the Cat Who Fishes, Street of Bad Boys, Street of the Warmed Up, Street of the White Coats). "Street of the Martyrs" fits into the last category.

So who are these martyrs who deserved a street to be named after them? They seem to be everywhere. A pharmacy, a pastry shop, a bistro, a men's clothing boutique, and a mom-and-pop grocery store on the rue des Martyrs all have the word "martyrs" in their name. One of the street's most popular breads is the *pain des martyrs*, a large, crusty, big-holed, white-and-whole-wheat loaf that never turns moldy. The street is so proud of its identity that for Christmas 2014 its merchants invested about 14,000 euros, along with 6,000 more from the local city hall, in new decorative lights for the street, including a huge banner in white that proudly proclaims, "Rue des Martyrs."

The explanation about the martyrs turned out to be a long and complicated tale. The French are obsessed with history, partly out of a genuine affinity for the past, partly from a desire to cling to lost glory. Most people I asked had an answer to the question of how the rue des Martyrs got its name. And if they didn't have an answer, they had a well-argued theory. The French learn in childhood that constructing a beautiful argument is more important than which side to take. Only the most self-confident confess to ignorance.

About one-third of the people I have asked about the martyrs had their story down cold. The name is rooted deep in Christian history and is so fantastical that even fervent Catholics find it hard to accept. The street's martyrs are Saint Denis and his two companions, Rusticus and Eleutherius, who lost their heads for preaching the Christian gospel.

There are no surviving contemporary histories of Denis, only interpretations of his life over the centuries, none reliable. The dominant legend is set in the third century, when France was part of the Roman Empire. The pope sent Denis to what is now Paris to convert the pagan population to Christianity, at a time when Christians were a marginal cult. Denis built a church, hired the clergy, smashed pagan statues, preached the Gospel, and made miracles. In modern parlance, he was a rock-star missionary.

Alarmed that they were losing ground to Jesus, pagan priests imprisoned the three Christians for refusing to accept the divinity of the Roman emperor. Many versions of what happened next appeared over the centuries. Denis and his companions refused to die, despite enduring a variety of tortures in prison. The most gruesome account of the tortures is described in an elaborate but fanciful ninth-century biography commissioned by Emperor Louis the Pious, the ruler of the Franks, and written by Hilduin, the abbot of the royal abbey of Saint-Denis, outside of Paris. Hilduin cared less about the truth and more about the creation of a cult of a patron saint to beat all others. In his telling of the tale, tabloid-style, Denis and his companions were beaten, roasted on a bed of iron, locked up with starving beasts, trapped in a blazing fire, and tortured on crucifixes. As happens with martyrdom, the trio's luck ran out. To ready them for death, God sent Jesus and a multitude of angels to give them Holy Communion in prison. Then soldiers led them far from the city center, halfway up a hill north of the Paris city limits to Montmartre. They stopped before the Temple of Mercury at what is now the rue Yvonne-le-Tac, near the top of the rue des Martyrs. There, the executioners cut off their victims' heads, using blunt axes to maximize their suffering.

Still, Denis held on. In a great miracle, and despite being ninety years old, he raised himself back to life. He cradled his head in his long white beard, washed it in a fountain, and carried it four miles north, to where he wanted to be buried, all the while accompanied by a choir of singing angels. But the resurrection was only temporary. When he reached his destination, he surrendered to death once and for all. Hilduin's biography was so full of plot twists, spine-tingling drama, and miracles that it is no wonder that until the French Revolution, it was considered the most influential version of the life of Saint Denis.

As for Saint Denis's body, one version of the story is that he was buried at the site of his ultimate death by a pious but cunning Christian widow named Catulla. She is also said to have rescued the bodies of Rusticus and Eleutherius and reunited them with that of Saint Denis, so they all could rest comfortably together in peace. When the twelfth-century Saint-Denis Basilica was built there, it displayed what were believed to have been Saint Denis's remains in reliquaries encrusted with jewels.

The fate of Denis's head, meanwhile, became the subject of fierce debate in the Middle Ages. The clerics of Notre-Dame Cathedral claimed to have possession of his cranium; the monks of Saint-Denis insisted they had his entire head. The dispute ended up in a protracted, acrimonious public trial in the French Parliament in 1410; its outcome is unknown. Denis became not only one of the most revered saints in Christendom but also the patron saint of France. French kings and future saints, including Bernard, Thomas à Becket, Thomas Aquinas, Joan of Arc, Francis de Sales, and Vincent de Paul paid homage by walking in Denis's footsteps up the route that is now the rue des Martyrs. It may be illogical, but the devout pray to him to relieve their headaches. (He is also the saint to call on if you need to be freed from strife or cured of frenzy, rabies, or possession by the Devil.)

IN MY NEIGHBORHOOD, SOME people who know the legend sought to give it a rational explanation. Valérie Tadjine, the hairdresser at Franck Provost at the bottom of the street, said it was possible Saint Denis could have walked without his head. She described the chickens and ducks she saw as a child at her godmother's house. "I saw their heads chopped off, but sometimes their nerves didn't die," said Valérie. "They'd run as far as . . . I don't know . . . maybe as far as Montmartre!"

After a branch of the Belgian food chain Le Pain Quotidien opened on the rue des Martyrs, I asked Adeline Huré, a waitress in her twenties, if she knew the origin of the name. "Charlemagne came through here with the head of a decapitated king to the Saint-Denis Basilica," she said, with great confidence. "There was a big hill and it is said that this was the hill of the dead, so he passed by with the head."

"Charlemagne carried a king's head?" I asked.

"Yes, but I don't know if Charlemagne or someone else cut it off," she said.

François Perrocheau, the Pain Quotidien Paris district manager, began to laugh. "Wasn't the king Richard the Lion-Hearted?" he asked.

"Good try, but wrong!" I said.

Other people told me the name referred to victims in French history—most often the 1789 French Revolution, or the 1871 Paris Commune, the violent Socialist movement that briefly ruled Paris.

"Rebels marched down the rue des Martyrs from Montmartre during the Commune, and they were martyred, no?" said Juan Alarson, whom I met at a neighborhood fair at the place Saint-Georges.

His friend Marie-José Ballesteros contradicted him: "No, no, it had something to do with the Revolution. I'm sure of it, the Revolution."

Claudine Dumoulin, who was with them, said both were wrong. "It was the road that led to the battle of Montmartre in the Middle Ages," she said, inventing a battle that may never have happened.

Enzo Guénard, a teenager whose father is the owner and chef of the bistro Miroir at the top of the street, said he was sure it related to the suffering of the Allies at the hands of the Nazis. "It dates from 1939 to 1945," he said, sounding like a history professor. "The Germans tortured the Allies to learn about their secret projects."

I broke the news to all of them that the martyrs had nothing to do with wars in French history.

Sébastien Gaudard, the chef-owner of Pâtisserie des Martyrs—the haute couture pastry shop he opened in 2011—came close to the truth. He said the name referred to his namesake, Saint Sébastien.

"He was a martyr!" he said.

Indeed, Saint Sébastien was a third-century Christian proselytizer and martyr, most often depicted as a handsome youth shot with arrows. Not a bad guess. Not 100 percent correct, either. "Don't you have customers who wonder about the origin of the name?" I asked him. "I mean, you named your shop after the martyrs."

"The only origin my customers want to know is the origin of the strawberries and lemons in my pastries," said Sébastien.

The most creative explanation I heard came from an elderly

woman who said she had lived on "the street of married men" for forty years.

"What street is that?" I asked.

"The street of married men—the martyrs! People call the rue des Martyrs the street of married men because they are all persecuted by their wives."

I met my match—almost—in Bruno Blanckaert, a businessman who invested in the Miroir bistro. He said he had thoroughly researched the topic and found three explanations. "The first is that the name is linked to a religious congregation," he said. "The second relates to people who had been in prison on the rue des Martyrs. The third is what you find in the most authoritative text, *Dictionnaire historique des rues de Paris* (Historical Dictionary of the Streets of Paris), which states that nobody is really sure."

He argued with such precision that I hesitated to question him. Seeing my bemused expression, he asked, his voice filled with authority, "And you? Do *you* know the explanation?"

"I'll give you a hint," I said. "There was a martyr who was made a saint."

Bruno laughed. "Ah, you're not telling me right away."

"You should know this!" I said. "What if a client comes into your bistro and asks, 'Monsieur Blanckaert, how did the rue des Martyrs get its name?'"

"I will give my three explanations, because how do I know your answer is the right one?" he said.

"You want me to tell you? You really do?"

He did. And so I told him.

AS I PLUNGED DEEPER into the archives, I learned that the rue des Martyrs did not always have this name. As early as the eleventh century, the road walked by the three martyrs was known as chemin des Martyrs, or "path of the Martyrs." The path originated in the center of Paris and continued all the way to the top of the Montmartre hill; the present-day rue des Martyrs is toward the end of that path. Beginning in 1290, the lower part of the street became the rue des Porcherons, after a wealthy local family whose "village" included a large swath of what is now the Ninth Arrondissement. But the street was sometimes considered an extension of the rue du Faubourg Montmartre, which is how it is identified by the Turgot maps of 1734–36, a series of twenty highly accurate bird's-eye views of Paris. The name "rue des Martyrs" did not arrive until 1750—and it disappeared for thirteen years, between 1793 and 1806, when the French Revolution purged names evoking God, the Virgin Mary, saints, and angels. During those years, it was called "the street of the Field of Repose." Not until 1860 did the rue des Martyrs unite with the chaussée des Martyrs, its extension into Montmartre; in 1868 the rue des Martyrs as we know it was created.

The story of the "martyrs" became even more muddled after Zygmunt Blazynsky, caretaker of the crypt believed to be the site of Saint Denis's beheading, told me that Rusticus and Eleutherius, his sidekicks, may never have existed. He had no evidence either way, but I discovered more about them in a doctoral dissertation, *The Liturgical Faces of Saint Denis*, by Tova Leigh-Choate.

An American scholar who studied at Yale, she is one of the

world's living experts on Saint Denis. She wrote that Rusticus and Eleutherius probably weren't known before the seventh or eighth centuries—several centuries after they supposedly lost their heads. All I can say for sure about them is that they became saints and had streets in Paris named in their honor.

In fact, Saint Denis himself may not be who we think he is. There were multiple Denises in early Christianity, and their stories were conflated into one over the course of the Middle Ages. Denis Number One is Dionysius the Areopagite, a first-century disciple and convert of Saint Paul who is mentioned in the New Testament Acts of the Apostles. Denis Number Two is our Saint Denis, the decapitated, head-carrying, third-century martyr. Denis Number Three is a second Dionysius the Areopagite, also now known as Pseudo-Dionysius, a fifth- or sixth-century theologian of the East so caught up in mysticism that he dropped hints in his writings that he was Denis Number One. Denis Number Three was so convincing that Hilduin incorporated his writings into his ninth-century work on Saint Denis.

The whole truth may never be told.

"My personal thoughts are that a certain Dionysius missionary-bishop probably existed in the third century or later, and he may well have been martyred," Leigh-Choate said in a series of e-mail exchanges. "If he existed, surely he had disciples, whether their names were Rusticus and Eleutherius or not (probably not). The rest of the story . . . well, it's a good story."

Leigh-Choate said it doesn't really matter whether Rusticus, Eleutherius, or even Denis ever walked the earth. Their importance is their impact on history and what people have believed about them over the centuries. "Denis was one of the most important saints of the Middle Ages," she said. "The Christian identities of the kingdom of France and the French church itself were intimately linked with the Saint Denis story. But his star fell with the French Revolution and, frankly, he's not that revered any longer."

So were Denis—the idol-smashing, head-carrying preacher-saint—and his companions real? And if they were not, why couldn't the rue des Martyrs represent all of the martyrs of French history, even its married men?

SOME OF
MY FAVORITE
GHOSTS

...

Come with me down this street
and meet the ghosts of our earliest years.

—JULIEN GREEN, PARIS

*F*ROM TIME TO TIME ON THE RUE DES MARTYRS, I HAVE imaginary conversations with Thomas Jefferson. He knew this neighborhood well, and in the early morning as the damp night fog lifts, I am sure I can make out his ghost. It vaguely resembles Nick Nolte, who played Jefferson in that gilded 1995 Merchant-Ivory film *Jefferson in Paris*.

Jefferson found friendship and talked politics on the rue des Martyrs, and he cultivated an illicit love just a few blocks away. But he is only one of many ghosts on this street. They congregate at Le Dream Café, at No. 8. I can't prove it. But sometimes, as I sip a *café crème*, I feel their presence: a face stares from the foam in my coffee cup; a paper napkin flies off the table when the air is still; a cold wind brushes my cheek.

Some may accuse me of a self-indulgent imagination, or of

just frittering away too much time at a comfortable table at No. 8. But consider that Allan Kardec, who systematized and popularized spiritism, a way of talking to dead people, lived just above where I am sitting as I drink my coffee. Kardec was the pen name of Hippolyte Léon Denizard Rivail, a nineteenth-century French writer, educator, and translator. He spoke several languages and taught such subjects as mathematics, physics, comparative anatomy, chemistry, and astronomy. From 1855 to 1860, he conducted very unusual activities from his two-room apartment on the third floor of this very building.

At least once a week, Kardec hosted sessions for fellow believers with a medium who made contact with the spirits. He also had lively conversations at home, but not with just anyone. He talked to Socrates, Homer, Mozart, Benjamin Franklin, Swedenborg, Napoleon, and a gaggle of saints, including John the Evangelist, Augustine, Vincent de Paul, and Louis. I like to think the conversations were fascinating. "Tell me, John, how did it feel when you discovered that Jesus had risen from the dead?" Or: "My dear Emperor Napoleon, if you had to fight Waterloo all over again, what would you do differently?"

Kardec said "superior spirits" ordered him to write a book codifying his findings. *The Spirits' Book*, the first of his five-volume guide, was a best seller when it appeared in 1857. I picked up a copy of the much shorter, watered-down version of Kardec's opus, titled *What Is Spiritism?*, which appeared two years later and is still in print. I learned, alas, that spiritism could not help me predict fluctuations in the stock market; make my fortune; know the future; produce an invention ready to be marketed; or discover coal mines, lost inheritances, or hidden treasure.

Spiritism attracted famous followers, including Thomas

Edison, who tried to invent a machine to communicate with beings in the afterlife, and Victor Hugo, who wrote, "Turning a blind eye to the spiritist phenomena is turning a blind eye to the truth." Sir Arthur Conan Doyle, the creator of Sherlock Holmes, exposed himself to ridicule with his belief in spiritism. (Conan Doyle killed off Sherlock Holmes in 1893 to devote himself to writing about spiritism but brought him back to life years later because of popular demand—and a need for an income.)

Spiritism still has a healthy following around the world, particularly in Brazil, where millions of people believe in communicating with the dead and spiritism is treated as a respected religion. Spiritists there are called "Kardecists" and run day-care centers, libraries, clinics, hospitals, and retirement homes. In 2007, Brazil's National Congress named April 18 the National Day of Spiritism in honor of the first date of publication of *The Book of Spirits*. Spiritism has figured into the plots of Brazilian films, plays, and soap operas. I occasionally see guidebook-carrying Brazilian Kardecists in front of No. 8 rue des Martyrs paying homage to Kardec—and perhaps trying to make contact with deceased friends and relatives.

When Kardec died in 1869, he was buried in the vast Père-Lachaise cemetery, on the eastern fringe of Paris. His grave is unusual: his bust in bronze sits beneath a large stone replica of an ancient portal tomb. His followers believe they can make contact with the spirit world by placing their hands on the statue. The tomb is adorned with more flowers than any other at Père-Lachaise—quite extraordinary, considering that Chopin, Proust, Balzac, Oscar Wilde, Colette, and Jim Morrison are also buried there.

EVERY CITY HAS ITS FAMOUS GHOSTS. Paris, with its long history and enduring magnetism for artists and writers, has more than most. A surprising number of them walk the rue des Martyrs. I sometimes sense Kardec himself sitting next to me at No. 8 as I think about the stories, some tame, some exotic, of the well-known people who lived, died, worked, or played on the street. The headless march of Saint Denis up to Montmartre was only the beginning.

Could the small boy playing outside the hair salon and shoe repair shop at No. 40 be Maurice Ravel, the composer, who lived here for five years of his childhood, from 1875 to 1880?

Is that Honoré de Balzac, the prolific but financially troubled novelist, visiting his sister Laure at No. 47, where an American-style cookie shop opened?

Is the beggar on the rue des Martyrs at the corner of rue Hippolyte-Lebas the reincarnation of Paul Léautaud, an eccentric twentieth-century writer who lived on the street as a child? As an adult, Léautaud kept dozens of cats and dogs. Every day, dressed in rags and a hat, Léautaud asked the butcher, the baker, and the greengrocer for food to give his animals. Had he returned to his old neighborhood to beg?

The Carlos Cheio bakery and sandwich shop, at No. 65, opens early and caters to students at the high school next door. It stands on the site of the now-vanished neoclassical home of the Belgian artist Alfred Stevens. He displayed his exceptional art collection—paintings by Holbein, Géricault, Delacroix, Rousseau, Millet, Manet, and Morisot—and invited friends to paint views of his garden. He also ran a painting school with mostly female students. Parisian high society and great European and American art collectors clamored to visit. But in 1882, the house, with its large garden, was demolished in the name of progress, to be replaced by Hauss-mannian buildings and the newly created rue Alfred Stevens. If I had lived here back then, I hope I would have protested the change.

Do I see Pablo Picasso in the neighborhood? He lived for a brief time in 1909 in an artists' colony at No. 11 boulevard de Clichy, not far from the rue des Martyrs. In one of the first rooms in the Picasso Museum in the Marais, which reopened in 2014, hangs an oil painting in shades of gray, depicting the Sacré-Coeur Basilica in winter. It is an example of Picasso's early cubist work and, except for the rounded main dome, a riotous celebration of angles. Could he have painted it from somewhere on the rue des Martyrs? The museum reopening also drew attention to Picasso's inability to throw out the relics of his past. Among the two hundred thousand personal papers he left behind were cigar boxes with ticket stubs from cinemas, bullfights, and circuses, including the Cirque Medrano on the rue des Martyrs. (I discovered the existence of several circus ticket stubs during the Picasso-mania that accompanied the reopening of the Picasso Museum, when new details about his daily life came to light.)

Artists left their paint spatters all over this neighborhood. Delacroix lived and worked on the rue Notre-Dame-de-Lorette. Gauguin lived at the place Saint-Georges. Renoir, Cézanne, Van Gogh, Toulouse-Lautrec, Pissarro, and Monet all bought their paints from the celebrated Père Tanguy shop on the rue Clauzel off the rue des Martyrs.

Then there is the ghost of Théodore Géricault, most likely to be glimpsed on horseback. A painter who is considered the first of the Romantics and best known for *The Raft of the Medusa,* Géricault used his studio on the rue des Martyrs as a love nest. The best-known scandal involved his affair with his model Alexandrine, who was married to his uncle, a man twenty-seven years her senior. She bore Géricault a son, who was given up for adoption. After her husband learned of the affair, he kept her a virtual prisoner at their home near Versailles.

Géricault endured a very different suffering. In 1823, he fell off his horse on the rue des Martyrs and was badly injured. His health deteriorated, and he died a year later, at the age of thirty-two. Some people believe that the rue des Martyrs was named after his "martyrdom" on a horse. (According to another version, his death was caused by venereal disease.)

Musicians came here, too. Claude Debussy led songs and Erik Satie played piano at the rowdy cabaret Le Chat Noir on the rue Victor-Massé. Later in the twentieth century, Gabby and Haynes, Paris's soul food restaurant off the rue des Martyrs, served its spare ribs, honey fried chicken, shrimp gumbo, and kidney beans to Louis Armstrong, Lionel Hampton, Sarah Vaughan, Billie Holiday, Cab Calloway, Sidney Bechet, and Count Basie. If I listen hard enough, I can almost hear their music.

It is only logical that I feel the ghostly presences of the rue des Martyrs most strongly at Le Dream Café, at No. 8, not only because of Kardec, but also because the greatest concentration of ghosts in the neighborhood is across the street at No. 7. Any of them might be stealing my napkin or blowing me a kiss. Now a Carrefour supermarket, in the second half of the nineteenth century No. 7 was the Brasserie des Martyrs, one of the most famous Paris nightspots.

The Brasserie des Martyrs was not fancy. It had a large, glazed double door that led into a cavernous space lit with gas lamps. There was no sign outside, no frescoes or gilding or decorations on the walls inside except for a naïve painting of "King

Gambrinus"—the legendary patron of beer—raising a foamy glass. (The brasserie was famous for its beer.)

But it was also a place that defined literary bohemia. Some of the best artists and writers of the era gathered there, to have their reputations made or destroyed. "Each great man had his table, which became the nucleus, the center of a whole clique of admirers," wrote the novelist Alphonse Daudet in *Thirty Years of Paris and of My Literary Life* in 1888. "They were called Bohemians, and the name did not displease them."

The "thinkers" had their own table. ("They say nothing, they write nothing, they just think. . . . Bald heads, flowing beards, with an odor of strong tobacco, cabbage soup, and philosophy.")

At another table were the "smocks, berets, animal noises, rough jokes, punsters, crowded together in glorious confusion: those are artists, painters, and sculptors." The painters Courbet and the much younger Monet developed a close friendship at the Brasserie.

The writer du jour, Henri Murger, whom Daudet called "the Homer and Columbus of this little world," reigned over the central table. He had made his reputation—and a lot of money—on *Scenes of Bohemian Life*, an 1848 work that was first published in serial form and then rewritten as a play. Murger became prosperous enough to move to the rue des Martyrs from the other side of the river, and Giacomo Puccini turned his book into *La Bohème*, one of the most popular operas of all time. I'm certain their ghosts would visit if the supermarket played "Mi chiamano Mimi" over the loudspeaker.

Then there were the women, described by Daudet as "former models, fine creatures, but somewhat faded in appearance. . . . Curious specimens of a singular refinement, having passed from hand to hand, and caught from their thousand and one liaisons a veneer of artistic erudition. They express their opinions on every

subject, and according to the lover of the moment, declare themselves materialists or idealists, Catholics or atheists. Touching,
and at the same time somewhat ridiculous."

But more than any other, it is the ghost of the poet Charles
Baudelaire that hovers here. Baudelaire lived nearby on the rue
Pigalle, where he wrote critiques of art and music and used the
Brasserie des Martyrs as a sort of private club. He sat at Murger's
table, where he argued about art and drank too much. Daudet
described Baudelaire as "tormented in art by a thirst for the
undiscoverable, in philosophy by the alluring terror of the
unknown." He slowly poisoned himself with drink and opium,
contracted syphilis, became paralyzed, and died penniless.

Not everyone appreciated the Brasserie des Martyrs. "A tavern
and a cavern of all the great men without names, of all the Bohemians of petty journalism. Heavy, annoying, ignoble atmosphere"
is how the brothers Edmond and Jules de Goncourt, who lived
nearby on the rue Saint-Georges, described it in their *Journal* in
May 1857.

The writers of this stern judgment were not the first or the last
to see an "ignoble" side of the rue des Martyrs. The street became
even more infamous after Émile Zola, who lived for years in the
neighborhood, published *Nana,* his 1880 novel about the
depraved life of a Parisian prostitute. Zola's portrayal of lesbian
subculture was one of the first ever in mainstream European literature. He described a lesbian *table d'hôte* with a three-franc
dinner run by a "monstrous creature" of fifty named Laure
Piédefer and set it on the rue des Martyrs. In one crucial episode,
Nana's sexually ambiguous prostitute friend Satin introduces her
to the same-sex world by bringing her to dine at Laure's. They are
served the "old substantial dinner you get in a country hotel": puff

pastry *à la financière*, stewed chicken with rice, beans *au jus*, and vanilla cream glazed with burnt sugar.

If the food is unexceptional, the company is not. Nana is at first confused and repelled by seeing so many women having such a good time together. Satin slips away without telling her, presumably with another woman. Nana is left to pay the bill, and standing outside on the rue des Martyrs, "felt her bitterness increasing." But soon afterward, she is intrigued: "Her curiosity was even excited," and she began questioning Satin about "obscure vices." Despite her extensive sexual experience, Nana "was astounded to be adding to her information at her time of life and with her knowledge." Satin seduces Nana and becomes her lover—or, as Zola puts it, "her vice."

The ghost of Zola is a certainty of the rue des Martyrs; is Nana here, too?

Another ghost is Antonin Dubost, a senator for twenty-four years and the president of the Senate between 1906 and 1920. Why doesn't a plaque celebrate No. 10 rue des Martyrs, where he died? The ground floor of the building has been the site of a bakery since 1868. But Dubost didn't go there to buy baguettes. The upper floors housed a prosperous brothel for rich and powerful politicians, businessmen, even priests. One night after Dubost received what was described as a "special massage" from one of the women, he collapsed and died.

I collect old picture postcards. Sometimes I spend hours at Parisian antiquarian shops sifting through them, hunting for images— or, even better, messages—that speak to me. Sometimes the hunt uncovers more ghosts of the rue des Martyrs—and perhaps more evidence of its former reputation. Who was the polite gentleman who sent a postcard of the vast garden of La Providence, a former

refuge for the poor that is now a retirement home, to an unnamed "Mademoiselle" in 1924? He told her he would love to see her and introduce her to his friends when she returned to Paris from the United States. Who was the tortured soul, nicknamed Moune, who sent a postcard picturing the bottom of the rue des Martyrs to Toutou in 1906? She asked for forgiveness for not writing, said she would love him forever, complained about the high price of butter in Paris, and branded the rue des Martyrs a "nasty street."

Eventually I decided to tell Mahmoud Allili, the owner of Le Dream Café, about his building's special status in the world of Parisian ghosts. It was June 2014, and he was sitting at an outdoor table, waiting to greet customers for the France-Honduras World Cup soccer match that night. He had strung flags of the participating countries across the front of the café and was showing all the matches on huge television screens.

"Do you know that a very famous person lived here?" I asked him.

"All I know is that foreigners come here all the time and ask to take pictures in front of No. 8," he replied.

He said he found it amusing because the door is so plain—unadorned metal painted a shade of lavender. I told him about Kardec and spiritism, and explained that Kardec had lived on the third floor.

"So let's go in and see!" he said.

"You know the door code?"

"I live here."

Mahmoud punched in the numbers and led me and my daughter Gabriela to the end of a narrow courtyard. He pushed open the door and told us to follow. It was a simple entrance without an elevator. We climbed a dark staircase to a blue metal door on the third floor. "This," he said, pointing with a flourish, "is the door!" He posed so Gabriela could take a photo.

I was disappointed. It all seemed so ordinary—and I saw no ghosts.

When we returned, Mahmoud put a chair in front of the building's door. He sat down, crossed his arms, and posed again as the soccer match was about to begin.

"Wasn't that fun?" he asked.

I politely agreed with him. But now it was my turn.

"Did you know Gabriela played soccer in both the United States and France?" I asked, pumping myself up with motherly pride. "She played striker." That meant she was responsible for striking the most goals. "She was a champion."

Mahmoud thought he had heard me wrong. And Gabriela thought I was making too much of her youthful soccer career. But she played along. She took out her iPhone and found an action shot of herself at about seventeen, in her blue-and-white team uniform, her arms and long ponytail in flight, just as she was about to kick the ball. It was as if Mahmoud were seeing a pig fly. He burst into the Berber dialect of the Kabylie region of Algeria, where he was born, and shouted to his colleagues to come see an amazing feat.

After that, I had new standing at the café—as Gabriela's mother. But my excursion to Kardec's door with Mahmoud hadn't gained me any new knowledge about the café's ghosts.

SO BACK TO THE GHOST I began with, Thomas Jefferson. He arrived in Paris in August 1784, joining fellow Americans Benjamin Franklin and John Adams to negotiate trade treaties with

Europe. Nine months later, he succeeded Franklin as America's minister to France. His job was to represent the young republic at the tumultuous, dysfunctional court of Louis XVI.

Jefferson's move to France came at a difficult time in his personal life. His wife, Martha, had died several years earlier; and soon after he arrived in Paris, he lost his two-year-old daughter, Lucy, to whooping cough. Jefferson spoke mediocre French and was in poor health. But he adapted to the pleasures of Parisian life. Eventually he fell in love here, and so we have another ghost. Maria Cosway, exotic, golden-haired, beautiful, was an accomplished portrait and landscape painter, a harpist, a singer, a composer, and a deeply religious Catholic. She was also married—to Richard Cosway, a successful artist who attracted both mistresses and hangers-on.

Jefferson was entranced upon meeting Maria in the summer of 1786 (he was forty-three, she twenty-six). For several weeks, they spent just about every day together. Jefferson took her to the theater, to musical performances, and to gardens outside Paris. One evening, they went to a nightspot called the Jardin Ruggieri, on the rue Saint-Lazare, close to the base of the rue des Martyrs and just a short walk from what is now Le Dream Café.

The Jardin Ruggieri had originally been a vast private home and garden. After it fell into disrepair, the Ruggieri family—Italian fireworks experts who immigrated to France—transformed it, in 1766, into Paris's first amusement park. Here you could watch fabulous fireworks, enjoy pantomimes, stroll in the gardens, and dance under the stars. There was nothing subtle about the fireworks displays. The night Jefferson took Cosway, the program included "The Forges of Vulcan beneath Mount Etna" and "The Combat of Mars."

Cosway's husband ended the relationship by taking Maria to

London. But Jefferson could, for the time being, console himself with intellectual companionship. He had become friends with an interesting Frenchman with an estate on the rue des Martyrs.

The friend, with the unwieldy name of Chrétien-Guillaume de Lamoignon de Malesherbes, was a jurist, and one of the most important personalities of the reign of Louis XVI. Named minister of state in 1787, he proposed the establishment of a national assembly of notables, a new constitution, and a law creating administrative divisions by communes.

I have never found an explanation for why Malesherbes bought a country villa on undeveloped land so far from the calm elegance befitting his social status. It may have been his passion for botany and his determination to grow rare plants in his garden. For whatever reason, he was by far the most important resident then living on the rue des Martyrs.

Jefferson, more than two decades younger than Malesherbes, shared his passion for gardening, and the two became good friends. I can picture them strolling through the garden nursery, discussing seedlings and soil composition. Jefferson called Malesherbes "the most curious man in France" about trees, so they may have spent long hours debating the peculiarities of roots, barks, cross-pollination, insects, leaf blight, and fungal diseases.

Jefferson gave Malesherbes American pecans and cranberries he'd brought to France. ("The pecan is one of the trees of America that is the most interesting to transplant in Europe because its fruit is excellent and with a taste very different from other nuts," Jefferson wrote his French friend in 1786.) He also brought Malesherbes what he called a "prodigious quantity" of shrubs and trees. One of Jefferson's favorite trees was the Virginia juniper, whose seeds Malesherbes planted in his nursery.

The two had more in common than gardening. Malesherbes was a passionate supporter of American independence, religious tolerance, and freedom of the press. (He helped the philosophers Voltaire, Diderot, and Rousseau publish their writings, which had been banned in France.) He had a remarkable library, to which Jefferson contributed a copy of *Notes on the State of Virginia*, the book that laid out his views on religious freedom. Jefferson referred to Malesherbes as "the good and enlightened minister" who was "unquestionably the first character in the kingdom for integrity, patriotism, knowledge, and experience in business."

Malesherbes survived the first phase of the Revolution and in 1792 became the personal lawyer of King Louis XVI. For that service, Malesherbes was arrested at the end of 1793, at home on the rue des Martyrs. He refused to defend himself. On April 22, 1794, he was forced to watch as his daughter, son-in-law, and granddaughters were guillotined; he then followed them to the scaffold. The French state seized their properties and possessions (which were later returned to surviving family members). The house was torn down, and the site was eventually rebuilt as the Cité Malesherbes, the private gated street that it is today.

Despite the death of his friend, Jefferson strongly believed the French Revolution had ushered in an era of freedom that needed to be preserved. The deaths and destruction, while unfortunate, were necessary sacrifices to the higher cause of liberty. "My own affections have been deeply wounded by some of the martyrs to this cause, but rather than it should have failed, I would have seen half the earth desolated," he wrote.

I wonder if they ever spoke before Malesherbes was beheaded, if they parted as friends, or if Jefferson felt betrayed by Malesherbes's unswerving loyalty to the king and asked for his seeds back.

THE KNIFE
SHARPENER

...

As to knife sharpening, I am no expert.

—Julia Child,
letter on May 5, 1952,
to her friend Avis DeVoto

ONE DAY, A LIVING GHOST CAME TO THE RUE DES MARtyrs. It announced its presence with a bell. The sound, which got louder, pulled me into the past. The bell from Holy Angels Elementary School, perhaps? But no, a school bell ringer would not be moving around.

I followed the sound until I saw the bell ringer. He was a *rémouleur*, a person who sharpens knives on a grinding machine. This particular grinder was Roger Henri, and he pushed a two-wheeled cart with a narrow wooden seat. The cart had two wooden pedals and two grinding stones connected to a wheel. Pedaling turned the wheel, which turned the stones, which sharpened the knives.

In that moment I was back on the far West Side of Buffalo, where I had grown up in an immigrant neighborhood—or, more accurately, a Sicilian one. Ethnic Italian groups tended to cluster, so the Siciliani, the Abruzzesi, the Calabresi, the Campagnesi, and the Campobassani had their own areas. The far West Side, near the Peace Bridge over the Niagara River to Canada, belonged to Sicily.

When I was a kid, a knife sharpener walked through the neighborhood and announced his presence with a hand-held bell. Women circled round with their knives and scissors, many of them grateful for a few minutes out of the house.

Henri, the Paris knife sharpener, had a mustache and glasses and wore a long jacket with enormous pockets. He was a trout fisherman, which I perhaps could have guessed from the fishermen and trout decorating his suspenders. His big belly and a pudgy chin made him look older than his sixty-five years. He dispensed cream-colored cards in flowery script with the name and description of his business: "Maison Roger. All types of sharpening of tools, knives and scissors. House calls."

With work to do, Henri didn't much care for chitchatting. But when I asked if I had time to run home and get my knives, he perked up and followed behind me with his cart. I brought him seven big kitchen knives and two pairs of scissors from my apartment. He couldn't escape my questions now.

Henri had learned his trade from his mother. For fifty years he had been trolling the streets of Paris with a cart custom-made by a locksmith. He left it in the courtyards of buildings where he knew the concierges; when it was time to change neighborhoods, he transported the cart in a small truck. He did business in just about every part of Paris, and worked every day except Sunday. "Sunday belongs to the Lord," he said.

I asked why he had stuck with the business. "I'm independent," he said. "I have no one behind me giving me orders."

I asked whether all the pedaling tired him out, and he said,
"Noooooo," as if it were a ridiculous question. "I pedal even
when I'm not grinding. Heh. I'm pedaling now while I'm talking
to you."

It is rare to see a knife sharpener in Paris. Chimney sweeps
and chestnut sellers still roam the streets with pushcarts from
time to time. But most itinerant workers—rag pickers, glaziers,
china repairers—are long gone.

This special moment of freelance craftsmanship needed to
be shared. So I told everyone who passed that we had a knife
sharpener in our midst. Now, if I were in New York City and
asked people to move closer to a man holding knives, they
might think I was a lunatic and call the police. And if I were in
my old Paris neighborhood off the rue du Bac, people would
give me a disdainful stare that said, "You are vulgar, foreign,
and do not belong."

But this is the rue des Martyrs, where people are more relaxed.
Plus, I am respectable-looking, it was the first sunny day of
spring, and just about everyone was in a good mood. Further-
more, Ilda Da Costa, the concierge in my building, who knows
everyone in the neighborhood, was just as interested as I. She
stood by my side and gave me credibility.

"This is like old times," said an old man. "It's like when I was
five years old and someone would cry out in the streets, 'Sharpener! Knife sharpener!' And we'd come down with our knives.
It's fantastic! We ought to make a film."

A woman said, "This is so rare! Hardly anyone does this anymore!" Her knives needed sharpening, but she lived in a fifth-floor walk-up and had arthritis. I volunteered to get them for her, but she glared at me as if I were crazy, or maybe a potential thief, and said thanks, but no thanks. I gave her my phone number in case she changed her mind.

Another man stopped and said he was an artist. He gave me postcards of two of his paintings, scenes from Montmartre. By this time Henri had finished sharpening and was eager to leave. I told him I had lots more knives. I ran upstairs and found a dozen antique knives with bone handles and carbon blades. The blades were stained black.

Hah! That would keep him busy.

Henri chided me for having exposed the knives to humidity, the enemy of sharpness. "Never, ever expose carbon blades to dampness!" he said.

While Henri worked, Pierino Anselmo, the Italian-born glazier whose shop is two doors down from my building, came by. He was so excited by the sight of the knife sharpener that he launched into a personal story in rapid-fire Italian. He said he came from a long line of glaziers. His family immigrated to France to find work after World War II. Two of his great-great-grandfathers, his grandfathers, his parents, and several of his uncles had been itinerant glaziers. He had opened his shop more than fifty years ago, when he was in his early twenties. But from the age of fourteen until then, he had been a street artisan, like the knife sharpener. He walked with a heavy wooden contraption filled with glass plates strapped to his back, shouting, *"Vi-trier! Vi-trier!"* "Gla-zier! Gla-zier!"

"People opened their windows and signaled me to come in," he recalled. And on the spot, using only a glass cutter, a ruler, a small hammer, and putty, he replaced their broken windowpanes.

Pierino was among the last of the family to sell replacement glass on the street. "The craft no longer exists," he said. He has a black-and-white photo of his uncle on a street in his hometown of Turin, with his glass carrier on his back. His shop, Miroiterie Vitrerie de la Victoire, is still a family business: Pierino works with his niece, Sophie Anselmo, who manages the shop. They have two trucks and five employees, who travel around Paris working on construction projects and for private companies. "I want to be known as the most beautiful glazier of Paris," said Pierino.

A neighbor in my building, Jean-Claude Lalou, came by with a handful of knives. That gave Ilda the push she needed. She brought a small knife from her kitchen and joined the conversation. "This will last how long, what you are doing to my knife?" she asked.

"More than a year," Henri said proudly. *"Ah bah oui.* Otherwise it's not worth it."

She was skeptical.

"More than a year, my little woman," Henri said again. "It's the same whether you use it once or you cut with it every day."

Ilda wanted to know why knives don't stay sharp for a whole year after you buy them. "It's mass production," he said. "Industrialization."

I announced that I knew a thing or two about knife sharpening, that I had two whetstones and two sharpening steels my father had given me when I was just starting out in life.

Henri called them worthless. He said there are rules governing stones: you need to know when to oil them and which side to start on; as for steels, they help to maintain, but not improve, the sharpness of the blade.

Finally, it was time for me to pay Henri: "Two hundred euros," he announced. Two hundred euros? The price of a pair of decent leather boots? To sharpen a few knives? He explained that each knife costs twelve euros, each pair of scissors seven, and that he was giving me a big discount. I looked at my antique knives. I had paid twelve euros for the whole set. Still, in sharpening them to perfection, Henri had removed their black stain. They shone bright silver in the sun.

GUESS WHO'S COMING TO PASSOVER?

...

To know people, to gain their confidence,
to know their private lives, even their vices
and their villainous stories.
To write everything.

—PAUL LÉAUTAUD,
WRITER WHO LIVED AS A CHILD
ON THE RUE DES MARTYRS

*F*OR GUY LELLOUCHE, THE GOAL IS LESS ABOUT MAKING money and more about appreciating lovely objects. Guy usually wears a gray felt fedora, velvet pants, dark glasses, and, when it's cold, two pashmina scarves. He has been an antiques dealer for decades, accumulating both the eccentric and the rare: an eighteenth-century silver Russian box, nineteenth-century rose-cut diamond earrings, mid-twentieth-century metal chairs.

His shop is halfway between my apartment, on the rue Notre-Dame-de-Lorette, and the base of the rue des Martyrs. He keeps it lit all night. The warm yellow glow exposes the curves and angles of furniture and sculptures, so that details lost by day suddenly proclaim themselves in the darkness.

He is about sixty but can look older or younger, depending on the day. His wife died several years ago, so he now shows off photos of his only child, a daughter, and his young granddaughter. On one level, he is provincial. He speaks no English and has never been to the United States. He longs to visit the Museum of Modern Art in New York but knows he will never go.

Guy is the product of two cultures, Europe and the Middle East. His grandparents hailed from Egypt, the Netherlands, Tunisia, and Italy. He embraces the identity he brought to France from his native Djerba, in Tunisia. But he is as straight-talking as an American, and he fills his stories with dramatic flourishes worthy of the stage.

He is so knowledgeable about art and antiques that he would fit right in with the high-class dealers on the rue du Dragon or the rue de Seine in Saint-Germain, across the river. In his shop I once saw a marble-topped table with an elaborate bronze base that was wrapped for delivery to the residence of Princess Caroline of Monaco; her decorator is one of Guy's longtime clients.

In good weather, Guy leaves his front door open to entice customers to enter. Or he moves the shop outdoors. One day he lined up, on the sidewalk, six Art Deco walnut dining room chairs upholstered in leopard-print velour. He sat on one, as if to say, "Please join me." Another day he put out a metal crate of heavy white cups and saucers marked with the name "Cafés Richard," for the giant French coffee-roasting company. He was selling them for fifteen euros apiece and planned to throw out the leftovers at the end of the day. Instead, he gave them all to me.

I don't know if Guy makes a living; I know he has fun. At

four p.m. most days, Guy invites clients and neighbors to join him at his shop for tea and conversation. One day as I passed by, he held up an empty gilt picture frame, as if to frame his smiling face. I cannot walk by without saying hello.

Guy is Jewish and wants everyone to know it. Even though he is only occasionally observant, he seasons his exclamations with Hebrew. The French have a reverence for the secular republican state that makes them keep religion to themselves. But as soon as we met, Guy revealed himself. Maybe it's because I'm American, and we Americans tend to be more straight-to-the-point than the French. Or maybe it's because my husband is Jewish and that makes me an extended member of Guy's tribe.

The conversation started the day I spotted a silkscreen in the window of his shop. It looked like a jubilant Miró with two flying menorahs. I walked in, introduced myself, and said I had a question.

"Are those menorahs?" I asked.

"Ah," he replied. "You must be Jewish!"

"Actually, I'm not," I said. "My husband's Jewish; I'm Catholic."

That didn't sound right to Guy. If you're not Jewish enough to marry a Jew and not Catholic enough to marry a Catholic, how can you be attached to your religious identity, he wanted to know.

Suddenly, I was telling my story: how Andy and I met by chance early one Saturday morning on the Long Island Rail Road en route to New York's Hamptons, how we had been at different stages of our lives and in different worlds and never would have met otherwise, how we fell in love but were believers in our own religions so conversion was out of the question, how we were married in a joint religious ceremony by a rabbi and a Jesuit priest.

"Nothing happens by chance," he said.

"You mean it was *bashert?*" I asked. I was using what I thought was a Hebrew word (one of the few I know) meaning fated or "meant to be."

Except the word isn't Hebrew, it's Yiddish, and Guy is not an Eastern European Ashkenazi but a Tunisian-born Sephardi. He had no idea what the word meant, so I told him. He said he liked my spirit. And even though he had not met my husband, my loose connection to Judaism through him was all it took for Guy and me to start an ongoing conversation about life, love, family, religion—and the exquisite objects in his shop.

Our relationship involved the oddest things. One day we began an exchange of goods, what the French call *le troc*. Guy was delighted when I gave him a large, ornate, silver menorah of unknown origin that I had found in a cupboard while cleaning out my office at the *New York Times*; I was delighted when he gave me a bottle of old wine he had rescued from a client's wine cellar. It leaked around the cork and smelled of vinegar. But what vinegar!

When I bought a lithograph of an abstract landscape by Nicolas de Staël from him, he slashed the price without my even asking. I thanked him with a gift of four English bone china stands trimmed in gold; long ago, menus were handwritten on them for each formal dinner, then rubbed off for the next time. He scribbled useful information about the shop on them and put them in the window.

One day I complimented him on the Hermès scarf he was wearing.

"What Hermès scarf?" he asked.

"Your scarf," I said. "It's an Hermès."

Guy was wearing a scarf of the softest of silk in shades of peach and gray. It was knotted loosely. The ends were tucked into his striped shirt.

"It's not an Hermès," he said.

"Bet it is," I replied.

He whipped it off, and sure enough, there was the word *Hermès* written in script. The edges were hand-hemmed with the hem rolled on the outside—a dead giveaway.

"Maybe I should give it to you," he said.

"Great," I said. "And why not take mine?"

I happened to be wearing my least favorite Hermès. I had bought it about twenty-five years before, late one night at the airport in Shannon, Ireland. Those were the days when I was covering Secretary of State George P. Shultz, who was struggling to inch the Middle East peace process forward. The 1960s-era 727 in which we traveled couldn't fly nonstop from the Middle East to Washington, so we refueled at Shannon. The duty-free shop was opened especially for us, and after ten days of too much work, too little sleep, and the haze of two Irish coffees, I couldn't resist an Hermès, not even one patterned in shocking pink, lime green, violet, and lavender. It was much newer than Guy's, and the silk was thicker and less supple. It belonged on a country club golf course in Connecticut. I hardly ever wore it.

I took it off and gave it to Guy.

"I love it!" he said. "This is my shade of purple. It goes great with my blue eyes."

"It's yours," I said.

So I took his Hermès, and he took mine. We double-knotted them around our necks. We were happy.

When I slipped off my new scarf that night, I noticed the artist's signature along the border: Henri d'Origny.

Henri d'Origny! I know him. He has been a designer for Hermès for decades. He and his American-born wife, Sybil, are friends of mine.

I looked up the scarf on the Internet. Sure enough, Henri designed it in 1963, one of his more than one hundred Hermès scarves. It was issued in eight colors: two shades of blue, two shades of red, turquoise, ivory, and mauve, as well as the one that was now mine, in peach.

The next time I saw Guy, I was wearing the scarf. I told him about Henri and his designs for Hermès. "What a coincidence!" I said.

"There's no such thing as coincidence in life, my dear Elaine." There it was again—the power of destiny.

Now whenever I wear that square of peach silk, I think of two of the most important Frenchmen in my life: Guy and Henri.

OVER TIME, GUY AND I peeled back the outer layers of our lives. Our leaps into intimacy were episodic. Like the time he almost lost the Miró (yes, it was a Miró) silkscreen I loved. One day, he closed the shop at lunchtime and left it outside.

For a brief moment, I was tempted, very tempted, to take it home. Not to steal it, but to hold on to it for safekeeping—and also teach Guy a lesson. Of course, I'd eventually tell him about it. Maybe he'd be so grateful that he'd give it to me for free.

Instead, I took the Miró into the sandwich shop next door. The manager kept it safe until Guy returned.

The next time I saw Guy, he told me, "Alas, a friend is sometimes like a *fiacre*. You can never find one when it rains. You're not like a *fiacre*."

I had no idea what a *fiacre* was or what he was talking about.

He explained that a *fiacre* was a kind of carriage. I still didn't get it.

"Okay, a friend is sometimes like a taxi," he said. "You can never find one when it rains. You're not like a taxi. You're a faithful friend."

Guy would tell me stories about growing up in Tunisia. Once he found a file of random family photos and, one after another, showed them to me: a studio photo of his grandfather as a teenager in Tunis, dressed in a suit and tie and leaning against a formal armchair, a Jewish temple as the backdrop; Guy at age forty posing in front of the bright blue gate of what had been his kindergarten in Tunis; a barefoot belly dancer wearing a beehive on her head and boredom on her face as she danced at Guy's bar mitzvah; Guy and his daughter about fifteen years before, surrounded by pink peonies on a terrace of their country house in Normandy before his wife died and grief drove him to sell it.

I told him stories about my past and my own wobbly faith, which sprang from sixteen years of Catholic education—twelve with the Grey Nuns of the Sacred Heart and four with the Jesuits. I have always liked the idea that negotiating with God, either directly or through the Virgin Mary and the saints, just might trigger divine intervention. That's how I tried to find God again in the fall of 1983. President Ronald Reagan had sent the marines to help calm Lebanon's civil war. They were drawn into the country's partisan morass and came to be seen as participants rather than peacekeepers. I was a roving international correspondent for *Newsweek*. The Beirut bureau needed reinforcements.

The fighting was so intense that the Beirut airport was closed. The only way to get into the country was to sneak in: relatively safely by ferry across the Mediterranean from Cyprus or dangerously by car overland from Israel.

I am subject to motion sickness. Not just ordinary motion sickness but the debilitating kind that keeps me off every ride at an amusement park. Traveling on a slow-moving aircraft carrier requires massive doses of Dramamine. Swinging on a swing? Torture. An all-day ferry ride over the choppy Mediterranean? Never.

I flew into Tel Aviv, hired an Israeli driver, crossed the border into Lebanon with an American passport and no visa, hired an Arab driver, and headed north. Somewhere outside of Sidon, on the road to Beirut, the shelling started. I had no idea what the target was, or if there was a target. But shells were landing on both sides of a desolate road, so close that the smell of explosives filled our lungs. The driver wanted to turn back. I refused.

This was long before cell phones. I had no way to communicate with the outside world. I mentally took stock of the situation: *I work for a weekly news organization and no one is waiting to hear from me. I'm going to die with this panicked driver; vultures will attack my corpse before anyone knows I'm dead.*

At that moment I thought of Saul on the road to Damascus. And I made a pact with the Almighty. "God," I said, "If you get me out of this, I'll believe!" (If truth be told, I said, "I'll try hard to believe.")

A few hours later I was in Beirut, in a comfortable room in the Commodore Hotel, where foreign journalists stayed. Shortly after I left, a few weeks later, suicide bombers blew up separate buildings housing American and French military forces, leaving 299 people dead. I had been at the American barracks just days before. Maybe God *was* looking out for me.

I told Guy that after this act of terrorism, I was trapped. I had promised God I would believe. I was superstitious and Sicilian enough to know that I had to keep my promise. Guy knew that even though I wasn't Jewish, I was a worthy interlocutor.

Guy and I built a relationship of trust strong enough that one day he lent me a necklace for a black-tie event. I was planning to wear my black-tie-event uniform: a red silk Dior-style dress. It needed a necklace. Guy had the perfect one in his window, a gold-plated choker from the 1950s, delicately worked and flat against the skin. It was priced at 280 euros.

I told him I couldn't justify spending that kind of money on a bauble. A fancy tasting meal for two in a Michelin-starred restaurant? Maybe. A piece of costume jewelry? Never.

"So wear it for the evening!" he said.

I was tempted to make a joke about Guy de Maupassant and his twisted tale "The Necklace," but I knew Guy Lellouche was superstitious. I took the necklace and kept quiet.

I returned the next day with the necklace and a box of chocolates.

Then I asked if he had ever read "The Necklace."

"Of course," he said. "Everyone knows that story."

It is a dark tale about a woman of little means who borrows a diamond necklace from a friend to wear to a fancy event. When she loses it, she borrows money and buys a replacement without telling her friend what happened. She and her husband spend years working to pay off the new necklace. At the end of the story, the woman runs into her friend, and she learns that the necklace was fake. All the hard work and sacrifice were for naught.

I told Guy that in the story, the woman had lived on the rue des Martyrs. She really did. "She could have been our neighbor!" Guy said. He laughed and laughed.

One year I invited myself to his apartment to break the fast of Yom Kippur, the holiest Jewish day of the year. Many Jews follow the rituals of the high holidays even if they don't keep kosher, observe Shabbat, or consider themselves "religious." They fast without food or drink for a full day, beginning at sundown the evening before; on the Day of Atonement, they go to synagogue to pray.

The eighteen-year-old Jewish daughter of a friend was staying with us during the Jewish holidays. She wanted to have a rich cultural experience in Paris. I signed her up for an English-language Yom Kippur service. But what to do about breaking the fast? Andy was out of town. The pressure was on.

Guy! I came right out and asked if we could join him. I knew he wouldn't say no. To turn away a practicing Jew on the highest of holy days would have been worse than rude.

Guy's apartment is on the ground floor in what was once a shop that sold motor oil. It is a modest space: a studio with a kitchen in the back; a narrow staircase leads to a sleeping loft. The apartment's high ceilings provide plenty of wall space for him to hang dozens of paintings from his inventory, one above another.

He was proud that he had prepared the meal himself. First came a special drink made with lemon and honey; then pistachio, almond, and pine nut cake with quince jelly; then an egg-and-ground-chicken terrine.

Guy told us stories about Tunis, where people go from house to house to break the fast with family and friends. He said fasting made his legs ache, that the set of plates for the terrine dated from the late eighteenth century, that important French personalities had reserved places in his synagogue. He said that according to legend, the El Ghriba synagogue in Djerba was built on the site where a modest, pious, and beautiful young Jewish woman lived alone in a wooden cabin. One night her cabin was devoured by fire. She died in the blaze, but her body miraculously did not burn, and she was proclaimed a saint. Guy said she performed miracles. Her specialty was to make barren women pregnant.

A Jewish saint—who knew?

THEN ONE DAY GUY was gone. A handwritten sign on the door announced that his shop was closed indefinitely. There was a number to call, but I didn't recognize it and didn't call. I didn't want to hear bad news.

Slowly news seeped into the neighborhood that Guy had suffered some sort of attack and collapsed. There was no word on whether he would recover. I summoned the courage to call the number on the door and was patched in to his cell phone. His voice was slow and quiet. He had injured his back. He was in constant pain and would need surgery.

Months later he returned, twenty pounds lighter and what

seemed like ten years older. He had abandoned his air of casual elegance for the comfort of a velour jogging suit. But Guy being Guy, luck kicked in. He put on weight and began buying and selling again. He looked better than ever. One day he announced, "No operation! Four doctors say yes, and two say no. I'm going with the two who say no."

His biggest problem was where to celebrate Passover. While he was in the hospital, his apartment had flooded. The insurance companies were still wrangling over who should take responsibility for the repairs.

"You'll come to us," I said.

We never seem to have enough people to fill our table, and certainly not enough who are familiar with the Passover story, the Seder plate, the yarmulkes, the table settings, and the Hebrew songs. Andy was pleased. He always leads the reading of the Passover story, the prayers, and the songs, navigating between English-Hebrew and French-Hebrew Haggadoth, depending on the linguistic talents and limitations of our guests. I take care of the food.

Guy came with his daughter, his granddaughter, and his special Tunisian Seder dish: beef simmered for fifteen hours with beans, eggs (still in their shells!), and Tunisian spices. The long, slow cooking turns the whites of the eggs a purplish brown. It was so special that Guy insisted it had to be served as a separate course—after the gefilte fish, matzo ball soup, and osso buco (my touch) and before the flourless chocolate cake. Jean-Claude Ribaut, one of France's most important food critics and another of our guests that night, proclaimed the dish "Excellent!"

"You are like my little sister," Guy told me on the way out.

That intimate designation came with responsibilities. One day Guy said he had a favor to ask. His daughter had never married.

"Could you find her a husband?" he asked. "He doesn't even have to be Jewish."

THE
MURDERED
SCHOOLGIRLS

. . .

To our martyrs, victims of Nazi barbarism
who died for France. Tortured, deported,
gassed, killed on the way or during bombings.
To forget would be to betray.

—Memorial plaque
at the Edgar Quinet school
on the rue des Martyrs

WHEN TERRORISTS STRUCK PARIS IN JANUARY 2015, leaving seventeen victims and three jihadist gunmen dead, the neighborhood mourned. Merchants up and down the rue des Martyrs taped black-and-white signs with the words *"Je suis Charlie"*—"I am Charlie"—to their windows; it had become the universal slogan of solidarity with the satirical newspaper *Charlie Hebdo*, the terrorists' first target. Police armed with machine guns were stationed in front of a five-story Haussmannian structure on the rue des Martyrs, the residence of Patrick Pelloux, an emergency room doctor and part-time *Charlie Hebdo* columnist who survived the attack. Residents welcomed the officers' presence; even the preschoolers who were required to open their backpacks for inspection made small talk with them.

Among those killed were four Jews who had been taken hostage by one of the gunmen in the second target, a kosher supermarket on the fringe of Paris. That Friday evening, the Grand Synagogue of Paris, a few blocks from the rue des Martyrs, canceled its Shabbat services, the first time it had done so since World War II. The synagogue, the largest in Paris, had long been under police protection. Now more police officers armed with machine guns arrived as reinforcements, and new metal barriers were erected.

Before the attack against the supermarket, many of France's Jews were already becoming uneasy about their place in the country. In Paris in 2014, anti-Semitism returned with new ferocity. Jewish groups recorded double the number of verbal and physical acts against Jews that year than the year before. In mid-July 2014 at the place de la République and in immigrant neighborhoods of Paris's suburbs, for example, protesters shouted three ugly, evil words: "*Mort aux juifs!*" "Death to Jews!" A week later in Sarcelles, one of the Paris suburbs, youths protesting Israel's military attacks in Gaza destroyed a Jewish-owned pharmacy. They showed no fear, only hatred.

France doesn't know how many Jews (or how many Muslims) live within its borders. The country's reverence for *laïcité*, which more or less translates to "secularism," means that questions about race, religion, and ethnicity are not asked in the national census. The best estimate, according to American Jewish organizations, is that France has close to five hundred thousand Jews. Only Israel and the United States have larger Jewish populations.

More than four million and up to six million Muslims live in France out of a total population of sixty-six million. France's history of anti-Semitism and its collaboration with the Nazis during World War II still cast shadows over the country's political landscape. Charges of anti-Semitism cut deep.

French prime minister Manuel Valls struggled to give this anti-Jewish phenomenon a name. He called it a new "normalized" anti-Semitism that "blends the Palestinian cause, jihadism, the detestation of Israel, and the hatred of France and its values." After the 2015 attack, he sought to assure the country's Jews that they belonged. "Without the Jews of France," he told the National Assembly, "France would no longer be France."

WHEN VISITORS THINK of Jewish Paris, they think first of the Marais, which has been a center of Jewish life since the Middle Ages. The rue des Rosiers in the Marais was once Paris's main "Jewish street." An ambitious urban renewal project that began in 2004 transformed it into a gentrified pedestrian walkway. Most of the Jewish shops and restaurants have given way to designer boutiques, restaurants, and bars.

There are other Jewish enclaves in Paris: Belleville and La Villette in the northeast, where Jews from Germany and Poland settled in the nineteenth century; the suburb of Sarcelles, where the Jewish pharmacy was torched, which is known as "Little Jerusalem" because it is home to about fifteen thousand Jews; and my neighborhood, the Ninth Arrondissement, which has seven synagogues (but just four Catholic churches). In the 1880s, Jews fleeing pogroms in Eastern Europe settled in the Ninth and other parts of Paris. North African Sephardic Jews came later, from Tunisia, Morocco, Egypt, and Algeria, because of the Arab-Israeli conflict following the creation of the state of Israel in 1948; a second wave arrived after decolonization.

Today the main Jewish area in the Ninth is southeast of the rue des Martyrs, where the rue du Faubourg-Montmartre, the rue Cadet, and the rue Richer intersect. On Friday evenings and Saturdays until dusk, Orthodox Jews wearing yarmulkes and prayer shawls walk in and out of neighborhood synagogues. The rue Richer, famous for the Folies Bergère theater, is the neighborhood's main Jewish shopping street, with kosher food stores, a bookstore, restaurants, bakeries, and a chocolate shop. Some of the signs are in both French and Hebrew.

Although the rue des Martyrs has no kosher shops, you can find its Jewish spirit at the bottom of the street. The Carrefour supermarket stocks various kinds of matzo, halvah snacks, and candles for Shabbat. Joseph Amiel, who owns the Orphée jewelry shop, is a Jewish émigré from Tunisia; so are the florists running the outdoor flower shop off the rue des Martyrs on rue Hippolyte-Lebas.

The Grand Synagogue, with eighteen hundred seats, is the architectural jewel of the Jewish community in Paris. Opened in 1875, it was a symbol of the rising power, influence, and high standing enjoyed by the Jewish bourgeoisie during much of the nineteenth century. The family of Emperor Napoleon III donated the land; the Rothschild family, an international banking family with ties to European nobility, largely financed the construction.

The entrance is on the narrow rue de la Victoire, not on a grander and better-trafficked street. Napoleon III's Spanish-born wife, Empress Eugénie, did not share her husband's affection for Jews and disapproved of an entrance to a synagogue between two nearby churches: Trinité and Notre-Dame-de-Lorette. So the synagogue is oriented north, not east toward Jerusalem, as it should be.

The foyer, grand staircase, and gilded candelabra are done in ornate Second Empire style. With its soaring facade, high nave, and enormous organ, the synagogue has the feel of a cathedral. Light streams into the ninety-two-foot-high sanctuary through circular stained-glass windows. A Hebrew inscription from the Book of Genesis announces, "This is none other than the house of God, and this is the gate of heaven." The synagogue looks European and familiar, not Moorish and foreign. Like the Eiffel Tower and Notre-Dame Cathedral, it has been classified as a national monument worthy of preservation. Former president Nicolas Sarkozy attended Yom Kippur services in 2006, when he was interior minister. Earlier that year, then-president Jacques Chirac participated in a memorial service at the synagogue for Ilan Halimi, a twenty-three-year-old Jewish man who was kidnapped, tortured, and murdered in the Paris suburb of Bagneux by a gang whose members called themselves *les barbares*. It was believed that Halimi was targeted because he was a Jew.

President François Hollande and Israeli prime minister Benjamin Netanyahu came here in 2015 for a ceremony honoring the memory of the Jewish victims of the supermarket attack. In his remarks, Netanyahu refrained from urging French Jews to leave France and settle in Israel, as he had done before. He was more subtle, noting that all Jews today are "blessed" with the right to live there together with their Jewish brothers. Later in the ceremony, some people in the crowd shouted, *"Vive Israël!"* and others followed with *"Vive la France!"* The Israeli national anthem was sung, followed by "La Marseillaise." And, as is the custom, the congregation asked God to protect the French Republic. The message of the synagogue is clear: the Jewish community is integrated into the fabric of France.

THE EDGAR QUINET HIGH SCHOOL nearby on the rue des Martyrs is similarly assimilated into French daily life. Yet it also bears witness to France's collaboration with the Nazis. Once a public school for girls, it is now co-ed. It occupies the original three-story structure built in the late nineteenth century on the site of a private home, and there is still a garden with trees and rosebushes in the back. It is named after Edgar Quinet, a nineteenth-century French writer, philosopher, and historian who advocated free, secular, obligatory education for both sexes. His book collection and personal papers, including an exchange of letters with Victor Hugo, sit in a bookcase in the principal's office. The school has a history of service to the French state. During World War I, the girls sewed bandages and clothing for the soldiers to wear in the trenches, and the soldiers sent back letters of thanks.

The outside of the school has been sand-blasted so thoroughly that its buff-colored stone seems to shine. The interior is run-down, with chipped, yellowing paint on the walls and bare parquet floors. Many students have ethnic roots in Arab North Africa, black sub-Saharan Africa, and Sri Lanka and come from working- and lower-class enclaves in the nearby Eighteenth Arrondissement. With few exceptions, they study technical subjects and trades.

Every year during his four-year tenure as principal until 2014, Jean-Claude Devaux hosted a ceremony of remembrance for the nineteen female students and one teacher who died during the

Occupation. "To our martyrs, victims of Nazi barbarism who died for France," says a large memorial plaque in the foyer. "Tortured, deported, gassed, killed on the way or during bombings. To forget would be to betray." Although the plaque, which lists all the girls' names, has been in place since the end of World War II, it took fifty years for a French president—Jacques Chirac—to acknowledge the country's role in the deportation of Jews and to formally apologize.

Scores of Paris schools have similar plaques. In the Ninth and Eighteenth Arrondissements, the Nazis deported about six hundred Jewish children to death camps. However, this plaque is unusual because the word "martyrs" is written in the feminine—*martyres*—because Edgar Quinet was still a school for girls in the 1940s.

The rue des Martyrs could have been named for them, for Fernande, Andrée, Blanche, Jacqueline, Huguette, Renée, Fanny, Marguerite, Lucienne, Louise, Alice, Lucette, Denise, Alice Rose, Lina, Éliane, Suzanne, Germaine Louise, and Madeleine Anne-Marie. The teacher is listed only by her last name: Dreyfus. Three died at Auschwitz, three at Ravensbrück. How the others perished is unknown.

One year I attended the remembrance ceremony at Edgar Quinet. I had expected a formal presentation in the auditorium, with all the students, where perhaps we would hear readings from Anne Frank's *Diary of a Young Girl*, or a concert by the school chorus. Many of the students face discrimination in their daily lives, and I thought they would be moved by tragic stories of genocide and inhumanity.

Instead, the commemoration was a modest, intimate affair. Bouquets of peach-colored roses still wrapped in cellophane sat on the floor below the plaque. Three students and a handful of teachers and administrators represented the school. A dozen elderly "Quinettes," members of the alumni association, joined them. The night was damp and cold, and none of us took off our coats.

"We pass by this plaque every day, and too often we forget to look at what is written here," Devaux told the group. "Every day we see the names of the martyrs on the rue des Martyrs. We have a duty to remember these girls—they were all girls—and their teacher, who were sought out and taken away to be killed."

His message grew more urgent. "It is now our responsibility and yours, young students, to tell others they must remember so that it will never again be possible for police to come into our classrooms as hunters," he said. "French police came to hunt down French girls, classmates of women who are with us tonight. Be vigilant so that it never happens again. Because anything is possible, always, always. You students must transmit the message to your generation that you must not discriminate, that you must not differentiate, that there can be no killing for religion or skin color."

He called for a moment of silence. Then he asked the elderly women if they knew anyone named on the plaque. No one spoke at first. Then, one after another, the women began talking.

"My mother knew Blanche's family."

"Lucienne was in my class."

"Lina and I went on vacation together. And Huguette was in my class."

"Germaine Louise and Madeleine Anne-Marie were sisters who joined the Resistance."

The women recalled the two-day *rafle du Vél' d'Hiv'*—the massive roundup of Jews who were brought to the sports stadium called the Vélodrome d'Hiver—in July 1942. Because it was summer vacation, the Jewish students from Edgar Quinet were taken with their families from their homes. One of the Quinettes at the commemoration recalled that the wailing of women and children had echoed off the buildings on the narrow streets as they were led away. When the roundup was over, more than twelve thousand Jews, including more than four thousand children, had been arrested in the city of Paris.

Lucienne Roudil recounted, without emotion, the story of her father, who had been a volunteer in the French army. He was deported to the internment camp at Drancy, outside Paris, where he died in 1941. Lucienne quit school at seventeen to help support her family. "I had the good fortune to be spared," she said.

Madeleine Kahn said she had been visiting her grandmother in Romania during the summer of 1939. When the Germans closed the border, she, her grandmother, and her aunt were forced to relocate to a remote corner of Romania. Her grandmother died, but Madeleine was hidden by nuns and reunited with her family after the war. "The generations that came after us, yes, it's hard for them to understand and learn from it," she said.

Devaux thanked his guests and invited us upstairs for a reception. We followed in silence and sat around a long table in an unadorned conference room lit in bright fluorescence. "Who wants a hot drink?" he asked. No one replied. Tea or instant coffee was not what they had in mind. He tried again.

"Who wants something cool and refreshing? Something bubbly?"

Ah, yes, they murmured. He poured a budget brand of champagne into flutes, and when there weren't enough to go around, a teacher fetched water glasses.

The women talked about mass killings of Jews in Ukraine during the war and how, even now, that horror is not fully known. They agreed that the Poles and Romanians had been more anti-Semitic than the Germans, and that anti-Semitism in Poland is still widespread. They lamented that too many young people today are indifferent to the Holocaust. One asked whether Jesus, born a Jew, would have been deported to a concentration camp if he had been living during Nazism.

Then, perhaps because of the champagne, perhaps because they themselves had survived, or perhaps because the trauma of remembrance was too painful to sustain, they turned to other subjects: the television series *A French Village*, about daily life during the Nazi Occupation; the injustice of the surveillance of private citizens around the world by America's National Security Agency; the impossibility of having a typewriter repaired these days; the magic of the iPad.

Life goes on.

I NEVER WOULD HAVE talked about religion in my proper, refined neighborhood off the rue du Bac. But along the rue des Martyrs, religion is a natural part of life. Stories emerge when you least expect them. One day I met with Jean-Michel Rosenfeld to learn about the Jean-Jaurès Foundation, a scholarly organization named after the founder of modern French socialism. The foundation is run out of a building in the Cité Malesherbes, the private gated street halfway up the rue des Martyrs. Rosenfeld worked for forty years as a special counselor to Pierre Mauroy, a Socialist leader who was prime minister for three years in the early 1980s under President François Mitterrand. "I was with Mauroy when he died," Rosenfeld recalled. "I closed his eyes for the last time."

Although he is retired, Rosenfeld serves as the foundation's volunteer spokesman. He told me the complicated story of the building. It was constructed as a private home, then transformed into a single-room-only residence, "the kind of place where lonely people live." Rosenfeld lowered his voice and added, "It is believed it was also a house for extramarital assignations." During World War II the Nazis requisitioned the house. "The bastards," he said. "One version of the story is that it became a private bordello for German officers."

After the war, the Socialists worked in secret here. Mitterrand himself came on a regular basis before he was elected president in 1981.

"If only these walls could tell their stories," said Rosenfeld.

Our conversation meandered, and he began talking about the Nazi Occupation. And Jewishness. His Jewishness. "It's such an honor for me, a descendant of poor Jews from a miserable Polish shtetl, to have been awarded the Legion of Honor," he said. "And I was interviewed by Steven Spielberg for his film *Schindler's List*. I'm in his archives!"

Rosenfeld was five and living in Paris when his father left in 1939 to fight with a French unit of mostly Jewish soldiers. His father was captured and imprisoned by the Germans. Rosenfeld said that when the Nazis occupied France and then began deporting Jews to death camps, he and his mother were allowed to stay in the country. "My mother was French, a Jewish Frenchwoman, and my father was a prisoner of war," he recalled. "There was a law that protected the wives of prisoners, as long as they were French. If they were foreigners, they would be deported."

Without money for a hiding place in the countryside, they remained in Paris throughout the war, wearing yellow Stars of David that identified them as Jews. They had little money, food, or heat, but they survived.

Every day, Rosenfeld wears a badge of honor in the left lapel of his jacket: a small red rosette that signifies his status as an *officier* of the Legion of Honor. But that was not the emblem he wanted to show me now. "I always have with me—" His voice stopped in mid-sentence.

He opened his wallet and pulled out something wrapped in clear hard plastic: a six-pointed yellow cloth badge with the word *Juif* in faux Hebrew lettering. Bits of black thread hung from the edges where the badge had once been sewn onto his clothing.

The Nazis forced Jews in Germany and its allied and occupied territories to wear identifying badges of shame. In France, the order took effect in the spring of 1942. Hitler's "Final Solution" was moving forward, and Louis Darquier de Pellepoix, French commissioner for Jewish affairs and a fanatical Nazi loyalist, announced that Jews would be required to wear yellow badges on the left side of their outer garments. Violators risked severe fines and imprisonment.

I had seen stars like this at Yad Vashem, the Holocaust museum and memorial in Jerusalem. But up close, this one seemed huge. Rosenfeld laid it in his hand and turned it over to reveal how it had been sewn. He smiled and lifted it in front of the left pocket of his suit jacket to show how he had worn it as a child.

"I am an old man, and when I die, I want to be buried with it," he said. "I'm not even observant. But I wore it every day to school until the end of the war. It has never left me. It's part of my life."

Rosenfeld was quiet, then said, "There's still ink on it, from when I was at school." Indeed, the star was stained with tiny splotches of black. The fountain pen he used as a child and kept in his jacket pocket must have leaked.

AFTER THE 2015 TERROR ATTACKS, Rosenfeld joined a massive march of upwards of 1.5 million people in Paris to show unity with France, to honor the memory of those who had died in the attacks, and to defend the freedom of the press. Many marchers carried signs saying *"Je suis Charlie."* Rosenfeld saw that a small number of marchers wore signs that proclaimed something different: *"Je suis juif."*

He thought back to the grenade and machine gun attack on Chez Jo Goldenberg, a Jewish restaurant on the rue des Rosiers in the Marais, in 1982. He was working for Prime Minister Mauroy back then, and arrived at the scene within thirty minutes. "I am a citizen of France," he said. "I believed it then and I believe it now."

As a Holocaust survivor, he is not afraid of the rising anti-Semitism in France. "I understand that some Jews are worried," he said. "It is mostly the Sephardi. They didn't know the horrors of the Holocaust the way we Ashkenazi did. And many of them don't feel like they belong to France the way I do. I have complete confidence in my country."

Was Rosenfeld wrong in his assessment of the new anti-Semitism? Was he getting too old and weak to fight back? Or was it that, as a French Jew who had stared down death as a boy, he was determined to embrace life until the end of his days?

His optimism recalled Émile Zola's upon attending the wedding of the thirty-one-year-old banker Albert de Rothschild and his eighteen-year-old cousin Bettina de Rothschild at the Grand Synagogue of Paris. The synagogue, which had recently opened, was filled with tropical plants studded with red and white roses. As the grand organ played, hymns and chants were sung in Hebrew. "You can have no conception of the beauty of the singing," Ferdinand de Rothschild, Albert's brother, wrote in a letter about the service. The couple took their vows before a crowd of people from French high society, including politicians, business magnates, aristocrats, diplomats, and even royalty. More than two decades later, the atmosphere would sour. Zola would risk his future to defend Alfred Dreyfus, a Jewish army officer who had been falsely accused and convicted by an anti-Semitic military court of selling secrets to Germany. But on this glorious day in March 1876, Zola was hopeful.

"Seeing Paris, filled with wonder and respect, crowding into this synagogue, I thought of one thing, the hatred to which the Jews had been subjected during the Middle Ages . . . ," Zola wrote in a column for a Marseille newspaper. "But it must be added that time has marched on, that civilization and justice have gained ground."

CHEAPER THAN
A PSYCHIATRIST

...

Clothes mean nothing until someone lives in them.

—MARC JACOBS

*T*HE PRESSURE WAS ON. ARIANNA HUFFINGTON WANTED
to shop, but time was running out.

I won't pretend that Arianna, the head of the Huffington Post
Media Group, is a close friend. We had met only once before,
when I interviewed her just before the launch of the French version of the *Huffington Post*. She had hired Anne Sinclair as its
editorial director, a brash move. Sinclair, a veteran French journalist and the heiress to an art fortune, was better known as the
stand-by-me wife of Dominique Strauss-Kahn, the former head
of the International Monetary Fund whose hopes of becoming
president of France ended the day a chambermaid in a New York
hotel accused him of sexual assault.

Arianna hadn't wanted to answer all of my questions about
Anne. But we had bonded as fellow journalists and mothers of
daughters, and had struck up an e-mail and telephone relationship. Now she was in Paris again, she had looked me up, and we

were having brunch at the Café Marly, in the Louvre. She had brought along her younger daughter, Isabella, a student at Yale, and I had brought along my younger daughter, Gabriela, a student at Washington University. As we ate in a dining room of satin and velvet luxury, Arianna and I decided it would be fun to take our daughters shopping.

We had only an hour to shop before Arianna and Isabella had to head to the airport. Complicating matters was that it was Sunday afternoon, and France has laws limiting most Sunday afternoon shopping. The aim of the ban is to protect small merchants with small staffs that cannot or choose not to work on weekends. So both big stores like Galeries Lafayette and small, big-name boutiques are closed. An exception is made for shops in designated tourist areas—like the top of the rue des Martyrs in hyper-touristy Montmartre. I told the chauffeur to take us there.

The goal was to find something pretty and French for Isabella. Gabriela decided that we would try Maje, a trendy shop that is part of a small French chain with original, flattering, if overpriced clothes that appeal to younger women. The chain had not yet opened in New York, so Arianna and Isabella didn't know it.

With her tall, lean body, Isabella was easily transformed into a lovely *parisienne*. She walked away with two dresses and a top. Arianna was so pleased that she insisted on buying something for Gabriela, who chose a fitted, short-sleeved cherry-red top with a jewel neckline and a flared bottom. It remains one of her favorite articles of clothing.

After this we had only fifteen minutes left, but I wanted Arianna to find something special for herself. Feeling confident, I led her into a world of adventure and chance that comes with going secondhand. Taking my friends to secondhand shops on and around the rue des Martyrs is at the top of my must-do-in-Paris list. It comes before my tours of pretty, small gardens; lesser-known churches; and hidden corners of the Louvre. I love the feeling that comes with finding a well-tailored, decades-old navy gabardine jacket with a "Made in France" label (usually dating from the years before much of French clothing manufacturing moved to Hong Kong and China) for the price of a double espresso. Even more, I love consulting with a team of personal shoppers who enjoy good conversation and appreciate my passion for the hunt.

The four of us headed to the very top of the rue des Martyrs, to a secondhand clothing shop on the corner named Chinemachine. We were a world away from Didier Ludot, whose museum of a shop at the Palais Royal sells meticulously curated haute couture. Reese Witherspoon, Catherine Deneuve, and Sofia Coppola are among Ludot's clients.

At first glance, Chinemachine looks like just another low-end secondhand shop. Racks of clothing and shoes mix with vinyl LPs, bangles with papier-mâché maps of the Paris Métro, odd bits of fur, sunglasses. A patchwork of nude and fashion photographs is taped to the wall behind the counter, along with a note that says, "We're cheap, so you don't have to be." (In other words, no bargaining. You're already getting a great deal.)

But at Chinemachine, you don't have to sift through mountains of awful clothing that smell like mildew, dust, and mold in the hopes of finding a 1960s tango dress for under fifty euros. Here, every item has been steam-cleaned and pressed by a special machine. Clothing is color-coded and organized on racks according to type. There are always tango dresses.

The boutique is owned by Martine Chanin, a thirty-something American with a natural feel for business and an even better eye for fashion. A New York City native, she moved frequently with her family as a child, went to college (as my husband did) at SUNY Binghamton, in upstate New York, and settled in Paris in 2003 to study French language and civilization at the Sorbonne.

Long-haired, olive-skinned, tall, thin, and confident enough to wear a leopard-patterned jumpsuit with stiletto boots, Martine is one of the braver of the American women who have made their lives in Paris. She started out slowly. For five years, she lived in a dark apartment infected with black mold. "I would scrub all the black mold off the walls and it would be back in a week," she recalled. "But the apartment was cheap and I was working nights in a bar with no work papers, so it didn't really matter."

She began collecting good-quality, reasonably priced vintage clothing from sources in New York. She stored her treasures in garbage bags and plastic bins in her tiny apartment. Eventually she quit her night job, teamed up with a partner, and then opened Chinemachine on her own, taking over a 325-square-foot, low-tech space that had been a contemporary art gallery.

Launching a business as a foreigner proved daunting. She paid one lawyer what she described as a huge sum of money only to discover, when she arrived at the immigration bureau in the Prefecture of Police to collect her work papers, that she was very, very illegal.

"They said, 'You need to get out of here,'" she recalled. "They said, 'You need to get on a plane and go back to New York or wherever you're from and get a visa for your business, and then like in six months maybe you can come back.' And I was like, 'Nope, ain't gonna happen. I just started this business. No way in hell I can leave.'

"So I got a new lawyer. And the new lawyer said, 'Get married.'"

Which she did. She married her Swedish musician boyfriend, whose citizenship in a European Union member country gives her the right to live and work in France.

Unlike high-end consignment shops, called *dépôts-ventes*, which take items on spec, Martine pays cash or gives credit for everything. "Taking clothes from individuals on a direct cash payment basis is an American concept that didn't exist here," she said.

And unlike low-end secondhand shops, which often buy in bulk, Chinemachine rigorously examines every item before accepting it. The goal is to sell cheap and fast. "You can do high-end, but you really have to know what you're doing," she said. "So I get it in, get it out. Constantly bring in new stuff with bargain-basement awesomeness."

One cultural divide was that many French women, despite their reputation as avant-gardists of fashion, are quite conservative in their dress.

"I'm shocked at how unimaginative women—even young women—are when it comes to fashion," she said. "Every time French girls try on something different, they'll say, 'You have to be daring to wear this!' I'm like, 'Well, then dare!' I feel that the store brings a little element of surprise. And maybe, hopefully some teenager is going to come in and be like, 'Yeah, maybe I really just want to buy weird stuff that costs five euros.'"

Martine speaks slowly, never raises her voice, and seems unfazed by adversity, reacting calmly even when a Chanel coat walked out the door with a shoplifter one day. When confronted with a mountain of clothes, she turns ruthless. I've seen her reject full suitcases, leaving the wannabe seller disappointed and humiliated. She has turned me down, more than once.

"You have to harden a little, get a little tough," she said.

Toughness has helped Martine deal with the lost souls from the nearby single-room-only residence who wander into the shop from time to time. One regular is a singer-guitarist with a 1960s mind-set.

"He's always dressed in a sort of sixties style," Martine said. "He often talks nonsense, but it's all sort of sprinkled with the names of bands and how it's not the 1960s anymore. I think his mother was a singer in, like, the forties or fifties and she was really well known or something. When he's feeling good, he puts his dentures in."

She tells more stories: about the ex-con who threatened to take a coat without paying, the elderly woman who seemed ready to buy a gypsy-style skirt and then pulled a scam, the well-dressed adolescent pickpockets who carried tools to remove the anti-theft security devices from the clothing.

Serendipity rules. At Martine's, I have found a Bruno Magli silver-and-black leather evening bag (twelve euros), purple suede Charles Jourdan flats trimmed in black leather (fifteen), a strapless flowered Yves Saint Laurent sunbathing top (twenty), and a short-cropped Max Mara wool crepe blazer (twenty). Just before my birthday one November, my daughter Gabriela spotted a sheared mink coat, with chestnut-colored skins so soft and lightweight that the fur felt like crushed velvet. Now, I have never been a mink coat kind of gal, but at fifty euros, and with the dead of winter coming, I was delighted to accept it as a luscious birthday present from Gabriela and her older sister, Alessandra.

The best deal ever came the day I bought Hannah Vinter, the twenty-three-year-old daughter of a college friend, a welcome-to-Paris gift. A scarf with a red border and a lively pattern in olive, ocher, and teal called out to her from the two-euro bin.

When I went to pay for it, Olivia, the saleswoman, said it was five euros.

"But it was in the two-euro bin!" I protested.

"The tag says five euros," Olivia replied. "It's worth it."

I almost didn't buy it on principle, but I couldn't disappoint Hannah. When we examined it closely back home, we discovered that it was signed "Hermès." An Internet search identified it as a 1991 design called "Art des Steppes" by the artist Annie Faivre. Like the scarves that Guy Lellouche, the antiques dealer, and I had once traded, it had the hand-sewn edges with the hem rolled on the front side that proclaim Hermès authenticity.

The next time I was in the shop, I asked Olivia if she remembered the scarf. I told her it was an Hermès and asked whether the five-euro price tag had been a mistake. "Not at all!" she said. "It was a surprise. We like to do stuff like that."

Finding an Hermès scarf in mint condition for five euros is the shopping equivalent of winning the lottery: it happens only once. So I didn't tell Arianna the story; I promised nothing more than a bit of fun. We entered the store, and Dani Siciliano, an American singer-songwriter living in Paris, was helping out that day. I introduced them—first names only.

Chinemachine doesn't get many celebrities. About the most famous customers over the years have been the American comedian Natasha Leggero and the British singer-songwriter Jarvis

Cocker. Dani flashed Arianna a glance of recognition but pretended oh-so-discreetly that she had no idea who she was.

Arianna, it turns out, is as relentless in sniffing out bargains as she is in running one of the world's most successful online news aggregators. From the jewelry case, she chose two bold gold-toned 1960s-era chokers for twenty euros apiece. Then she spotted a ten-euro BlackBerry case in crocodile skin.

As we were about to leave, she saw a floppy straw hat in a soft yellow and taupe with a tiger-skin motif. She pulled it down low over her forehead and giggled. Arianna Huffington actually giggled. Okay, this wasn't exactly the felt fedora Garbo made famous in the 1930s, but like the Garbo hat, it did disguise.

Arianna loved it. "I'm going to wear it now!" she said. "Let's take a picture together behind the counter."

Dani hesitated. Shoplifting is rife at Chinemachine, and Dani explained that inviting clients behind the counter was forbidden. But Arianna wanted to be part of the Chinemachine team.

"Oh, come on," she insisted. "I want you in the picture, too."

An offer Dani could not refuse.

"She knows how to be a really good troublemaker," Dani recalled later.

The three of us posed behind the counter for Arianna's selfie. We said our good-byes. It made me smile to see Arianna Huffington, a wealthy woman with polished skin and lacquered hair, head off to Charles de Gaulle Airport in a chauffeur-driven sedan wearing a ten-euro secondhand hat.

I have more fun in store for Arianna if she comes to town and wants to shop again. We will stop by No. 86 rue des Martyrs at By Flowers and say hello to the Israeli-born Paul Cohen and his twenty-something French business partner, Jonathan Winnicki.

There are few fancy designer names at this shop (although I once found a forest-green cashmere Burberry jacket for forty euros). It's mostly clothes dating back to the 1960s and 1970s, many bought in bulk. You need time and stamina to discover gold.

Then we will go to the chicest shop on my secondhand tour: Troc en Stock, on the rue Clauzel just off the rue des Martyrs. The prices of the almost-new clothing are reasonable—about one-fourth to one-half of retail—and some items are real steals (a caramel-colored, soft-as-butter leather Fratelli Rossetti jacket for 140 euros and a Max Mara leopard-print silk blouse for forty).

There's no negotiating with Sophie Meyer, the no-nonsense owner who opened the shop two decades ago. So I've tried to seduce her by bringing her bits of Coca-Cola memorabilia, which I know she collects, from the United States. We have developed a relationship of mutual respect, although I would never, ever have asked her for discounts. And then she started giving them to me.

My friend Susan, who hates shopping and spends a lot more money on Grace, her black Lab, than on her clothes, gave in to temptation during a visit to Paris and bought an entire dress-up wardrobe here: two clingy Diane von Furstenberg dresses, one Marc Jacobs black silk sleeveless shift, and a print Prada dress for everyday wear—for about the price of dinner for two at a two-star restaurant. (It helps that she's somewhere between sizes 2 and 4.)

"We keep out the chain stores and preserve the feeling of neighborhood," said Sophie. "And we're cheaper than a psychiatrist."

I know Arianna will like her.

IN CELEBRATION
OF BOOKS

...

There are two things you don't throw out in France:
bread and books.

—BERNARD FIXOT,
FRENCH PUBLISHER

ON THE THIRD SUNDAY OF EVERY MONTH, A SMALL
band of retirees takes over a corner of the rue des Martyrs. It's
time for Circul'Livre, a volunteer operation dedicated to the
preservation of the book. The volunteers classify used books by
subject and display them in open crates.

The books are free. Passersby may take as many as they want
as long as they agree to an informal pledge to neither sell nor
destroy them. They are encouraged to donate their own castoffs
to keep the stock replenished. The volunteers affix a large sticker
bearing the words "Circul'Livre" to the cover of every book,
which curbs the resale impulse. The sticker is backed with super-
glue, which makes it virtually impossible to remove without
damaging the cover.

When I moved with my family to Paris, we left most of our

books in storage. But I hated being without them. Surrounding myself with books makes me feel smarter. As Circul'Livre's are free, I have become a bookaholic. I can arrive home with two shopping bags full of books. I hide them behind the living room couch if my husband is home, then cram them into corners of the shelves in our apartment. He calls it a sickness; I tell him collecting books is a lot cheaper than collecting Fabergé eggs or sixteenth-century Dutch prints.

I have found hardcovers of Henri Troyat novels, French versions of Reader's Digest Condensed Books (leather-bound and gold-trimmed), cookbooks from the 1980s, and half of a ten-volume first edition of love stories in French history. Biographies of Jean-Paul Sartre, Brigitte Bardot, and Joan of Arc. Novels by Jacqueline Susann, James Michener, and Ernest Hemingway translated into French. In exchange, I have given Circul'Livre English-language novels in paperback, museum catalogs, publishers' bound galleys, and years of *Foreign Affairs*. I know I get the better deal.

Circul'Livre was created in 2004 by a voluntary group in the working-class Twelfth Arrondissement. It now operates with teams in about eighty locations throughout Paris. According to its website, making friends is part of the exercise: "Circul'Livre is not satisfied with the promotion of reading; it is a powerful vehicle for social relationships in the neighborhoods."

You can give the French no higher compliment than to call them intellectuals. I once went to a cocktail party and asked a French woman her profession. "Intellectual," she replied. She was serious.

Circul'Livre is a group of intellectuals—not because they ponder Descartes or Rousseau in our neighborhood cafés but because they share ideas about books. They are masters of verbal seduction, at using passion and politesse to begin a conversation that doesn't want to end. Whether the subject is Diderot or turnips, Circul'Livre wants to talk about it.

We Americans often consider the French habit of verbal play a waste of time, because it doesn't go directly to the point. But that's precisely what makes this monthly event so much fun. It is about pleasure, not results.

Jérôme Perrin and Bertrand Morillon, Circul'Livre's self-appointed "hosts" for our local branch, provide much of the banter. One Sunday, Jérôme picked up a book called *Philosophical Commentaries* and said, "Here you go. Here's one for the beach!" Bertrand preferred the soft sell: "Régine Deforges! A great classic! Great to put you to sleep!" During the 1980s, Deforges became a best-selling author and was called the "high priestess of French erotic literature." She could print books deemed offensive because she owned her own publishing house.

One Sunday, Jérôme told the crowd it was payback time. "*Chouquettes!* Won't someone bring us *chouquettes?*" he asked. I ran over to the bakery and brought back two dozen small *choux* pastries sprinkled with sugar pearls. Jérôme gave me a double-cheeked kiss and handed me an espresso in a white Styrofoam cup.

The next Circul'Livre Sunday, I got so caught up in the frenzy of the book giveaways that I found myself on the volunteers' side of the tables. As I hawked English-language books, Jérôme suggested that I come to one of Circul'Livre's monthly meetings. But there are limits to acceptance. Andrée Le Faou, a retired office administrator and one of the volunteers, was not pleased. She took a long drag on her cigarette and said nothing. She may have even harrumphed.

Later in the day, I asked Andrée what was wrong. She told me that only official members can stand on the organizers' side of Circul'Livre tables. I had broken the rules. I told her I wanted to become an official member.

"We adore you, Elaine," she said. "But our numbers are limited."

So much for that.

FRANCE RETAINS A REVERENCE for the printed book. As independent bookstores crash and burn in the United States, the market here is healthier, largely thanks to government protections that treat the stores as national treasures. Grants and interest-free loans are available to would-be owners, and price-fixing reigns.

In France, booksellers—including Amazon—may not discount books more than 5 percent below the publisher's list price. With such a small discount, many customers prefer to shop in stores, where book-loving salespeople stand ready to offer advice and opinions. E-books (whose prices are also fixed) have yet to become a big market, except for the French classics, many of which can be downloaded for free.

There are three independent bookstores on the rue des Martyrs and five more on adjoining streets. L'Atelier 9, at No. 59, most closely resembles an independent neighborhood bookstore in the United States. It has large front windows organized by themes that change regularly. The brightly lighted interior has cozy spaces for lingering. The employees enjoy talking to customers and recommending their favorite books; *"coups de cœur,"* they are called. Still, there is only one armchair, reserved for visiting authors, not idle readers. And no latte bar.

My first bookstore contact on the rue des Martyrs was Guy

Bertin, who sells used and discounted books at No. 21, close to where Circul'Livre appears each month. He has been in business for thirty years but claims to be struggling, despite rent stabilization that keeps his costs low.

His store, Le Bouquinaire, is an oddball shop with unpredictable hours. A small sign just inside is aimed at potential pickpockets: "To avoid confusion, thank you for leaving your purses, backpacks, and heavy coats at the entrance." Shelves in the window near the counter hold Bertin's personal collection of miniatures: dozens of Playmobil men, Smurfs, and other tiny figures in molded plastic. Sidewalk display cases entice customers with one-euro used paperbacks and splashy new photography books: *Paris of Dreams, Paris Disappeared, Paris Unknown.*

Bertin does not believe in idle chitchat. He smokes a lot. His clothes hang on his thin body. Although he is bald on top, his hair grows thin and gray down his neck. For the longest time, I felt like an intruder in his shop, where he greeted me with the requisite polite *bonjour* more out of necessity than warmth.

"He's a survivor," said my friend Katia Kermoal, who lived on the street for years. As the founder of *Le Daily Neuvième,* an online newspaper for the Ninth Arrondissement, Katia knows just about everyone on the rue des Martyrs.

We stopped in one day, and she asked Bertin how he was doing.

"Terrible," he replied. "I'm ready to quit. It's the Chinese." He spit out his words. "They come all the time and want to buy my lease. They want me out."

"Well, let's keep you in business a little while longer," I said cheerily.

I said I'd give him some English-language books to boost his foreign-language inventory. I told him a tale of woe about the British edition of my last book, about how the British publisher went bankrupt without paying my advance. The warehouse was stuck with three thousand copies and said that unless I bought the entire stock, the books would be destroyed. I bought them, for about twenty-five cents each. Even with shipping to France, each cost less than a dollar. Did he want a few copies? For free?

I thought the story would soften him up, or at least show him that all of us were suffering from the revolution in publishing. He said nothing as his thin lips curled down. Intellectual seduction was getting me nowhere.

The next day I dawdled outside, flipping through books on the display tables. I picked up a hardcover first edition: *Le temps des amours* by Marcel Pagnol. It cost one euro.

Then I ventured in bearing gifts: a copy of my book *La Seduction* in French and four copies of the cheap British edition. I asked Bertin if I could sign the English-language copies. "Maybe you could make some money here," I said.

"A book for sale is not a book sold," he replied.

But he relented. "You can sign one copy. That way the buyer will feel special. To be correct, here's your payment." He gave me five euros.

"No, I'll take the payment in books."

"My books are too expensive for you, Madame."

But when I tried to pay him a euro for the Pagnol, he refused to accept it. "It's yours," he said.

For free? A small victory!

"I treasure first editions," I said. "This is fabulous!"

He told me to curb my enthusiasm. He explained that while in the United States hardcover books cost more than paperbacks, in

France the "hardcover" usually means a cheap book club edition printed on mediocre paper with a rough binding. "The Pagnol is worthless," he said.

Once I came by with six books I knew he could sell, including a new novel by Marc Lambron, a member of the Académie Française; a heavy tome on the relationship between Paris and New York by Marc Fumaroli, also a member of the Académie Française; a memoir by Eva Gabrielsson, the woman who had been the longtime partner of the late Stieg Larsson, the author of the Millennium trilogy; and a political analysis of Lebanon and its lessons for the Middle East.

He started to hand me six one-euro coins, saying, "I don't want to be in your debt."

"They're not for sale," I said. "Next time I choose a book, you can give it to me."

"It will be too expensive for you."

One day, I brought Bertin the catalog of a new Matisse exhibition still in its original plastic wrapper (retail price: thirty-five euros); a catalog from an exhibition at the Maison de la Culture du Japon à Paris; and the glossy coffee table book produced for the 2012 season of the Spoleto performing arts festival in Italy.

He apologized that he hadn't found new books on the neighborhood for me.

Then he remembered: a 1965 book club edition of *Connaissance du vieux Paris* (Knowledge of Old Paris) by Jacques Hillairet, an eminent historian of the monuments, buildings, and streets of Paris. The book cost thirty-five euros.

"There has to be something in it for you," he said.

I searched the index, and on page 436 I found a delicious factoid: in 1787 there were fifty-eight structures on the rue des Martyrs, twenty-five of them cabarets. Bertin told me to take the book home. Wait—the bookseller was giving me a book?

Not so fast.

"Keep it," he said. "For a few weeks."

Thierry Cazaux, the neighborhood historian, doesn't think much of Bertin as a true bookstore owner. He refers to him as a *soldeur*, a vendor of discount books. "He should not be called *libraire*," said Thierry; he explained that while the term refers to a person who sells books, being one "requires vast knowledge and expertise. A *libraire* offers advice about literature."

I couldn't disagree more. For me, Bertin is a *libraire* and more. He's a *libraire* who knows how to stay in business. I told him so one day. "I'm not a *libraire*," he said in protest.

"Sure you are," I replied. "Okay, you have all these popular cheap books outside, but your back room—it is filled with old treasures: about cinema, art, theater, history, music, architecture."

"Madame," he said, "that is the most wonderful compliment you could ever pay me."

LIBRAIRIE VENDREDI, NEAR THE TOP of the rue des Martyrs, is a classic Paris bookstore run by what Thierry would call a true *libraire*. Its front window is filled with books of philosophy and poetry so obscure that I almost expected to see a sign saying, "Non-intellectuals Not Welcome."

When I was a college freshman, my English professor told me I would never be more than a B student. I majored in history. I avoided the required fifteen hours of philosophy by substituting foreign languages, convinced I would never master Plato, Aristotle, and the others. The experience left scars. I would never call myself an intellectual. So for the first three years I lived in the neighborhood, I stayed away from Librairie Vendredi.

A bookstore has been in this building for more than one hundred years, giving Librairie Vendredi the feeling of another era. It is a sliver of a shop, so small I knew that if I ever went in, I would have to talk with the two women who run it. They would ask if I wanted help; "Just browsing" doesn't seem like a proper response in a place of such erudition.

The shop's one concession to modernity is an outdoor display of bargain books. Anyone can stop and flip through the selections without feeling inadequate. Most are either unusual or obscure—a catalog from a sale of Gustave Doré prints from 1990, a dog-eared copy of a minor Molière play.

But one day I saw a book of essays by the British novelist Zadie Smith. In English. For two euros. It was my ticket in! I entered the shop, money in hand, to meet owner Gilberte de Poncheville and her associate of fifteen years, Hélène Murat.

Librairie Vendredi is no more than 215 square feet, so narrow there is hardly space for an island piled high with books selected as favorites of the day. Shelves rise at least ten feet from floor to ceiling; ladders against the wall make the high books accessible. Hidden away in the back is a counter used as a desk.

Gilberte was unsmiling and unassuming; her glasses and dangling earrings gave her a fusty look. She wore jeans and a cashmere cardigan over a buttoned-up blouse. I don't think Gilberte knew about Zadie Smith, which made me feel better about being there.

I asked her about herself.

"I don't have much to say," she told me in a weary voice. "I do my work. I'm not amusing. I'm not a worldly person—nothing like that, you know."

Hmm, I thought, *maybe she's as intimidated by me as I am by her books.*

"Maybe she prefers books to humans," whispered Marie, my research assistant.

Because the shop opens at noon, I thought Gilberte and Hélène might be semiretired. Not so. They need mornings to read their books so they can properly advise their customers.

One day Gilberte showed me a recent copy of the London *Sunday Times Magazine,* with an article describing the rue des Martyrs as one of the world's great shopping streets. It included sweet little illustrations in color; Librairie Vendredi was featured in one of them. I asked Gilberte if I could borrow the magazine to make a copy. I was surprised when she said yes. When I returned with the magazine and a framed copy of the article for her, Gilberte did something I hadn't expected. She smiled.

Then she began talking. As a child, she had wanted to be a florist or a bookseller. Eventually, bookselling won out. Gilberte and her husband bought Librairie Vendredi in 1978 from a Romanian refugee who was retiring. The shop, which had opened around 1910, still had its coal-burning stove—and shelves of books black with coal dust.

Today Gilberte has ten thousand titles, about 40 percent of them new books. She arranges books alphabetically by author according to subject, but she does not label the shelves. You just have to know that the small section on the right is psychology and the big wall on the left is poetry. Because Gilberte is a poetry fanatic, that is her largest collection. "Classic, modern, it's all mixed together," she said.

Gilberte and Hélène don't spend much of their time on accounting, so they don't know whether they turn a profit. They don't use a computer. I'll say that again: they do not to use a computer to keep track of their stock. Nor do they have a card catalog. They keep all (or at least most) of the books in their heads. "We're the computers!" said Gilberte.

She scorns what she calls the "uniformization" of books: the same titles in all the bookstore windows. "The books are whatever we like. We are completely out of the best-seller circuit," she said. "The important thing is to be a reader and to stay close to my books and to find books that you don't find everywhere." Gilberte is the very definition of an intellectual—even though she denies it.

Journalists pride themselves on storytelling, and I am telling Gilberte's story despite her reticence. "I hate books of anecdotes," she said. "You can't say very much with anecdotes. Too many anecdotes—it means the author lacks inspiration. There is no writing. There is no style. There is no poetry."

She also dislikes practical books. "You won't find a cookbook here, or a travel book, or a diet book, or any book on well-being with a title like *Discover Your Inner Clown*. These sell really well in France. But they're not for us."

She does have a small section of children's books, mainly for clients who come into the shop with their children. It is an odd assortment on oddball topics, including a children's book by Marguerite Duras, most famous for *The Lover,* about her affair with a Chinese merchant in Indochina when she was about fifteen.

The shop has a reputation for "being rather alternative" in its philosophy section, where it has books on "situationism." I thought of the 1957 musical *Funny Face*; Audrey Hepburn tells

Fred Astaire she wants nothing more than to go to Paris and attend lectures on "empathicalism." I wondered if there was a correlation between the two. I was too embarrassed to ask, so I just said, "Why do you have books on situationism?"

"Why? Because of our taste, because we are like that," said Gilberte. "We can say that about all of our books. We have lots of books about the theater and movies because we like the theater and movies. And we're rather on the left here—we make no secret of it—so we have connections with thinkers who are slightly subversive."

I could see that. In front of me was a book called *Marijuanaland*.

France has hundreds, maybe thousands, of small publishing houses; Gilberte maintains connections with many of them. "They can no longer sell to the big chains," she said. "They do great work; we want to welcome them. We're getting old and we have no time to lose."

I asked her to identify the jewels in her shop. "Oh, there are so many I couldn't possibly tell you," she said. But then she rattled off a few: *Les impardonnables* by the Italian Cristina Campo, French translations of poems by the American Charles Olson, minor works by Henry Miller and James Joyce. Clearly, one person's castoffs are another's jewels.

Given all the disruptions to publishing, Gilberte has to wonder whether jewels outnumber castoffs. She survives now because her space is rent-controlled. "I will hold on, but who knows how long?" she asked. "And what will happen after I'm gone?

"I have the impression that this is a bookstore like no other. What a loss if it becomes a charcuterie."

THE ARTISAN
WITH THE
GOLDEN TOUCH

...

I'm not an artist. I'm an artisan. I invent nothing. . . .
If you can see the restoration, then it is a failure.

—LAURENCE GILLERY,
ARTISAN RESTORER

NEAR THE HIGHEST POINT OF THE RUE DES MAR-
tyrs, at the foot of the steep incline toward Sacré-Coeur, sits a
shop that belongs to the past. *"Dorure s/Bois"* reads the sign,
painted in rich red on the wooden storefront. It loosely translates
as "Gilding on Wood" and advertises a service: painting gilt on
wood. The shop is always locked; you must ring to be let in.
Because there are no fixed hours, you never know when the white
metal shutters will be closed.

A mirror in a hand-carved gold frame hangs above the door.
The large picture window displays assorted objects that have
been restored, including mirrors set in gold-leaf frames adorned
in waves and curves. A cherub with uplifted arms watches over
Jesus on the cross. In smaller letters, painted in yellow on the pic-

ture window, the shopkeeper advertises a second, more obscure service: "Putting mercury barometers in working order."

Behind the window display, a small showroom has more mirrors framed in gold. Rows of antique barometers hang on one wall. Everything is for sale, but no prices are displayed. There is no desk; the only sign of administrative organization is a small round table with a telephone, a notebook, and a few pens. Parked next to the table is an object that seems out of place: a silver-gray motorcycle, big and flashy, with the brand name Otello. A doorway at the back of the showroom opens into what looks like a workroom. Sometimes a slim woman of indeterminate age dressed a long white smock bends over a counter, working in solitude.

During my first two years in the neighborhood, I never went in. I don't know anything about layering gold leaf, and I wasn't in the market for a mercury barometer. But I was curious about the woman in the smock.

Eventually I rang the bell, and she answered the door. Her skin was lined with fine wrinkles, her dark hair pinned into a bun. A small gold crucifix hung from a chain around her neck. She wore jeans and a flowered shirt. I saw flecks of gold leaf on her hands. She could have been forty—or sixty (she was actually fifty).

Her name was Laurence Gillery, and she greeted me with a musical *bonjour* and a smile so broad that it crinkled the outer edges of her cheeks and eyes. She escorted me into her workroom, where light manages to penetrate an industrial skylight dark with years of soot. Simple tools hang on the walls: screwdrivers, scissors, chisels, saws, glue, paint chips, odd-shaped pieces of bubble wrap. She keeps wine corks in a box that once held a round of Camembert cheese. "You never know when you might need a piece of cork," she said.

In one corner I saw a modern store-bought barometer with springs but no mercury. Why did she have it, I wanted to know.

She laughed: "It's the only one that works!"

Gilding old frames and mirrors, she said, is the easy part of her job. She seals any cracks with glue, hand-sculpts missing pieces from odd bits of wood, and applies gold leaf. The gilding begins with ten layers of a primer coat made from rabbit-skin glue and a special white paint. After remodeling and chiseling the carved moldings, she applies an ocher-tinted glue to conceal places not covered by the gold leaf. Then come three layers of glue and rust-colored clay.

She polishes the object with a stiff brush and fine sandpaper, attaches the sheer gold leaves with a sable paintbrush, and burnishes some—but not all—of the gold with a curved agate stone. Finally, she applies a patina that blends in with the gold leaf. The goal is not perfection, since that would make the object look new.

"Gilded wood needs to be seen from a distance," she said. "If you look at it closely, you will see stains and worn spots. That's the point. If it's perfect, it's horrible."

Although Gillery enjoys restoring gilded wood, it holds neither mystery nor challenge for her, and many other artisans do it well. Barometers are different. She proclaimed proudly that she is the only artisan in Paris who repairs mercury barometers. "I am a fossil," she said.

Old barometers are hard to find but are valued by collectors and interior decorators as objects for display. Some come to Gillery from antiques dealers; others from clients who inherit them, sometimes reluctantly, as they have no idea what to do with them.

None of the dozens displayed on the walls functions properly. Restoring a barometer to working condition requires such a large investment of time that Gillery doesn't begin until she has a buyer.

An eighteenth-century barometer with a wooden face nearly three feet wide rested on the counter. It looked unfixable to me, but a Swiss businessman had bought it recently for about 5,000 euros.

"Now I'm going to show you how to make it work," she said.

AN ITALIAN, EVANGELISTA TORRICELLI, invented the mercury barometer in 1643. It has a glass tube with a stopper at the top and a mercury-filled reservoir at the base. The weight of the mercury creates a vacuum in the upper length of the tube. When atmospheric pressure rises, forecasting sunny, dry weather, the mercury rises. Falling mercury and pressure precede bad weather.

Mercury is toxic and especially damaging to the nervous system. Hatmakers used it in the nineteenth century, with results that gave rise to the saying "mad as a hatter." Many U.S. states ban devices containing mercury, even classic glass thermometers. The European Union restricts its sale but allows trade in "antique mercury-containing measuring devices," such as barometers, if they are more than fifty years old. Gillery assured me that mercury contained safely in a barometer poses no risk.

Gillery learned the craft from her father, but before he accepted her as his partner, he gave her a warning: "You come into this world as you would into a religious vocation. Be careful before you settle here. Work somewhere else for a while."

She apprenticed at various workshops and was so talented that at age twenty, she landed a job restoring furniture at Versailles. It was a secure government post—a job for life, with an extra month of pay as an annual bonus, a five-week paid vacation every year, and a generous pension at the end of her career. She could have been a colleague of the finest artisans in the most glorious showpiece of France.

She hated it.

She hated working with bits and pieces, assembly-line style, with no chance of following a project from beginning to end. She hated taking orders from bureaucrats. She hated the chatter and small talk of her colleagues, all of them women restricted to the finishing stages of restoration.

"I learned from my father to work on an object from start to finish," she said. "I learned to work alone. Ateliers, even the best ones, like at Versailles, are assembly lines. You do one process and then pass the object to someone else. It's depressing."

Gillery quit after a year and joined her father on the rue des Martyrs. When he retired, in 1984, she bought him out.

A purple velvet curtain hides a staircase leading to the small apartment above the shop where she lives with her husband, a professor of French literature, and their two daughters, both musicians. Once upon a time, just about all of the merchants along the rue des Martyrs lived above their shops. She is one of the last. The apartment is so small that her showroom doubles as a dining room for special events, like the party she threw when her husband became a full professor. In 2014, she celebrated thirty years here.

Wearing her rough linen smock that fell almost to the floor, Gillery stood at a counter bolted to the wall. She was restoring a hand-carved barometer in gilded lime wood, accented in pale green. It weighed ten pounds and was set in a frame of carved flowers, birds, and arrows. One needle pointed to the weather ("tempest," "strong rain," "good weather," "very dry"), while the other indicated atmospheric pressure. In the center was a thermometer that Gillery said was a Réaumur, with a temperature scale invented by the French scientist René Réaumur and used in France until the Celsius scale took over, in 1790. It sets the freezing point of water at zero degrees and boiling at eighty. She didn't know when the barometer had been made but called it "Louis XVI style."

"I always put myself into the era of the object," she said. "Then I speak to it. I study it. It gives me pleasure. I become part of it."

She turned the barometer over and, with a pair of pliers and a flourish, pulled out the rusty nails holding it together.

"Are you a carpenter?" I asked, surprised.

"I'm doing what's needed to get it going."

The doorbell rang, and she sighed. She assumed the role of a boutique owner. A woman with a timid air carried, as if it were a baby, an object wrapped in brown burlap and tied with rope. The woman was in her fifties and dressed in elegant blue. She unwrapped a mirror set in a silver-toned frame with so many curves, angles, and mosaic pieces that I wondered where it ever could have hung.

"This mirror is of the Régence era, beginning of the eighteenth century," Gillery said. "Between Louis XIV and Louis XV."

The woman looked pleased. She clearly wanted to sell it but was too embarrassed to start the conversation by talking business. So she told the story of the mirror: it belonged to her grandmother, it had once hung in her apartment, she had redecorated with contemporary furniture and the mirror no longer belonged.

"I'll give you fifty euros for it," said Gillery.

The low figure shocked the lady in blue. She said the mirror had been in her family for a hundred years.

"It's damaged," said Gillery. Her voice was flat as she explained that the wooden frame had to be repaired, the mirror cleaned and refurbished. Even fully restored, she said, it would be worth only a few hundred euros.

"Well, it's not worth it for me to sell," said the lady in blue. She picked up the mirror, the burlap, and the rope. *"Bonjour,"* she said coldly.

Gillery waited for her to leave before launching into a tirade.

"People want to sell and not restore their objects," she said. "That woman used to have antique furniture, and she's thrown it all away for the modern. I'm in a precarious profession. It's not easy. I have small mirrors for three hundred, four hundred euros. How many people spend that much money on shoes, or clothes? They live for the present. They pass on nothing to their children."

Gillery knows that her time is running out, not because of illness or age but because the materials essential to her work are disappearing. She held up a small weight, a part for a barometer, shaped like a teardrop. "A watchmaker made this," she said. "It has to be precise and perfectly balanced so that it moves properly. It is precious."

Her father bought two hundred weights like this one forty years ago. She has only a dozen or so left. No watchmaker wants to fabricate something so complicated. And the needlemaker has retired, so no one produces fine barometer needles anymore.

"Maybe I have five more years," she said. "I'll use my weights and my needles and then I will no longer be able to bring barometers back to life. A world of dead barometers. It's a loss, no?"

MINISTER
OF THE
NIGHT

...

Half good, half bad, half girl, half boy, half cod, half penguin
Me, I am Michou!

— "Michou's Song"

I NEVER THOUGHT I'D BECOME A MICHOU GROUPIE; HE
didn't seem my type. Who knew he would be irresistible?

Michou is well into his eighties. He styles his white hair into a
puffy bouffant and hides his eyes behind giant glasses. He dresses
in a dozen shades of blue—custom-made, electric-blue satin
jackets; cornflower-blue cashmere topcoats; blue patent leather
loafers; blue ties; blue shirts; blue-tinted lenses in blue glasses. He
radiates eccentricity.

To meet Michou, you head north on the rue des Martyrs and
cross the broad thoroughfare where boulevard de Clichy and
boulevard de Rochechouart meet. You have now entered his
world, the world of Montmartre.

Michel Georges Alfred Catty, known to all as Michou,

created the transvestite cabaret at No. 80 rue des Martyrs close to sixty years ago, long before the term "drag queen" was much used. He is not a caricature of seedy old Pigalle or bohemian Paris. He is a showman, a successful self-made businessman, a philanthropist, and a beloved pillar of the community.

The story on the street says Michou's cabaret was the inspiration for Jean Poiret's wildly successful 1973 play, *La cage aux folles*. The play is about a gay cabaret owner and his drag queen companion who put up a straight front for the conservative parents of their son's fiancée. More than one million theatergoers saw it in France; five years later, the play became a popular French-Italian film adaptation, using the same name. In 1983, the American team of Harvey Fierstein and Jerry Herman adapted it as a Broadway musical; in 1996, Mike Nichols turned it into a film called *The Birdcage*, starring Robin Williams as Armand, the cabaret owner, and Nathan Lane as Albert, his partner.

I have no proof that Michou was the model for Poiret's cabaret owner. When I asked him about it late on a champagne-sipping afternoon, he gave me a Mona Lisa smile. Burnishing his reputation is part of his shtick. "I am the last muse of Paris," he likes to say. "I am the best-known, the most-beloved homosexual of France." He craves attention, and when he saunters up and down the streets of Montmartre, people stop—to stare, to chat, to take a photo. Those who don't know him might laugh; those who do treat him like family.

Michou claims never to drink water, juice, or spirits, only champagne, lots of it. Mother's milk, he calls it. By six p.m. every

day he is holding forth with friends and hangers-on at La Mas-
cotte, an old-fashioned bar and bistro on the nearby rue des
Abbesses. "I sit out on the terrace and twenty people ask to take
a picture with me," he said. "How I love that! How I love to be
recognized! 'You are Michou? The real Michou?' they ask. Ah, I
adore it."

He is so much a part of Montmartre that in 2014 the neighborhood declared April 19 "Michou Day." A Paris website
invited "friends of Paris" to gather at the place des Abbesses to
create a Michou flash mob. It instructed participants to wear
freshly ironed blue shirts and impeccably coiffed hair. "It's time
to cry out your love for one of the most adorable representatives
of our beautiful capital, the eternal Michou!" said the website.
On the designated day, Michou made his way through the crowd
to the stage. "Montmartre! Well, this is my life and this is my
heart!" he exclaimed. "For me this is a great moment, a great
moment of friendship. . . . What a beautiful day. *Youpi!*" (That's
French for *Yippee!*)

FROM THE OUTSIDE, CABARET MICHOU looks like a Montmartre tourist trap from a bygone era. The entrance screams
cheap. A poster-sized illustration of a big-lipped, big-haired,
long-lashed, blond floozy hangs above a glass case of photographs of transvestite entertainers. Fake flowers and fake ivy sit
in pots on slim balconies on the floor above. I used to walk
quickly when I approached, nervous that at any time of the day
or night a customer full of liquor and lust might tumble out onto
the sidewalk—or onto me.

But the more I passed the cabaret, the more I was tempted to go in. Finally I called, and Michou invited me over. "Meet me now!" he said.

The windowless front door, in shiny midnight blue, is always locked. You ring, and if you don't look like a criminal, a hostess lets you in. The decor is low-tech. Dozens of gilt-framed mirrors hang on the walls, pieced together like a puzzle. Mismatched chandeliers and touches of neon here, Art Nouveau there, give the place a cozy, dated look. The stage is small, with an image of the blond floozy on the front curtain and a sparkly black backdrop behind. The sign above the stage, announcing, "Michou's Folies," looks as if it was painted by an amateur.

Framed photos on the walls bear witness to Michou's celebrity at his peak, long ago: Michou with Josephine Baker, Michou with Lauren Bacall, Michou with Jean-Paul Belmondo. And with Peter Sellers, Jacques Brel, Romy Schneider, Liza Minnelli, Gérard Depardieu, Sophia Loren, Jeanne Moreau, Serge Gainsbourg, Joan Collins, Jean Paul Gaultier, Alain Delon, Claude Lelouch, Johnny Hallyday, Paul Bocuse. There are several photos with the Chiracs, including one with then president Jacques Chirac in the Élysée Palace.

"Liza Minnelli—she comes here often," Michou said. "She sits on the bar, *on* the bar! Not on the stool. Diana Ross came twice. Joan Collins. Lauren Bacall. Claudette Colbert. Peter Sellers."

A wave of sadness washed over Michou, reminding him that this is the past. "It's my small museum now," he said of the photos.

The tables are covered with disposable paper over white linen tablecloths, to reduce laundry costs. The chairs are of the bentwood bistro variety, not plush velvet and gilt. The strobe lights resemble those in a 1960s American basement family room. Duval-Leroy champagne, a respectable brand, is served in strong, squat-stemmed flutes that are hard to break and easy to wash.

The doors open at eight-fifteen. Michou offers two fixed-price dinner menus, the "Menu Paris," with wine, for 110 euros, and the deluxe "Menu Michou," with champagne, for 140. Both come with familiar three-course fare like country pâté, rump steak with green pepper sauce and mashed potatoes, Brie cheese, and the tart of the day. The "emblematic *flamiche*," a puff pastry tart made with leeks and cream from Michou's native Picardy, is always on the menu. The price also includes a cocktail and coffee. The food is passable, not gourmet. The rump steak is a bit tough, the salad greens a bit wilted, the tart crust a bit mushy. The crowd doesn't come for the food.

Most nights, the cabaret sells out to a respectable-looking, down-to-earth, very French audience. They are hard-working, fun-loving people, many from smaller cities, mostly over fifty and untouched by the ennui that comes from too many years in Paris. The after-dinner entertainment is more PG-13 than R. "No vulgarity," Michou said with pride.

"No prostitution, no drugs, no sex acts," added Oscar Boffy, his artistic director. "This is a wholesome house." Indeed, I once saw a couple here with their six-year-old son; he posed onstage with some of the performers.

"I will never, ever call you clients," Michou says each night before dinner and the show. "You are friends! And you are about to experience a very beautiful show! Do you know that I've been here for almost sixty years!"

Michou eases the crowd into the "daring" show. Grégory, a male singer in a sheer, low-cut white T-shirt that shows off his shaved chest; tight jeans; and a patterned black leather jacket, is the opening act. No cross-dressing yet, just a lot of clapping and hip swiveling.

Grégory (he only uses his first name) leads the crowd in the *cri de guerre* of the evening: *Youpi!* The crowd shouts *Youpi!* and bursts into applause. Grégory claps long and hard, slapping his microphone from one hand to the other to make the sound louder. The crowd has no choice but to clap along.

After Grégory has won over the audience, he trains his gaze on one woman and sings to her, only her. He plunges into the crowd, prancing and revving up the reticent. He sings songs that Michou sang forty years ago. On the nights when he hasn't had too much to drink, Michou jumps out of his seat and waves his arms high in the air.

Then the show gets more daring. A bellboy (Oscar, his bright-red lips lined in black) and two hotel maids in red page-boys wear midnight-blue satin and sequins. The maids' fishnet hose complement their skimpy uniforms.

Next comes a star straight from Canada: Céline Dion in a white gown and a long blond wig. She drops the gown to reveal an impossibly slim body in a short sequined minidress. "I am so, so happy to be here in Montmartre tonight! Vegas is nothing compared to Montmartre, Montmartre and . . . Michou!" she exclaims.

Depending on the night, Jeanne Moreau might follow, in a shiny sequined coat and cream-colored scarf. Or it could be Sylvie Vartan, in a red sequined leotard under a white tuxedo suit.

Oscar becomes a campy Amy Winehouse with big hair, swilling from a bottle of J&B scotch between snorts of coke. Then he's Maria Callas as Violetta, singing "Sempre libera" from *La Traviata*, dressed in an impossibly large red ball gown, with a

beehive hairdo, diamond necklace, and bright red lips. The audience loves him.

Christian (a.k.a. Marie-Pierre), a waiter who has worked here for twenty-eight years, knows he is beautiful, with extraordinary eyes. So he adorns himself with false eyelashes, layers of shadow, eyeliner, and mascara. He moves the lashes up and down, slowly, to undress others with his gaze. He colors his lips in a dark shade of honey to avoid detracting from his eyes. Then he transforms himself into Cher in a fur-trimmed, gem-encrusted headdress and a robe that he removes to reveal much more.

An elegant blonde in a black wrap cocktail dress comes close to me. It jolts me to realize that it's my friend Oscar again. He mounts the stage to do a skit about Chantal Ladesou, a fast-talking, plainspoken French humorist. When Oscar finishes, he steps down into the audience, where he singles out a male client. He flirts. He kisses him on the cheek. The man is not amused, but everyone at his table howls with laughter.

There's more: Tina Turner, Marilyn Monroe, Whitney Houston, Lady Gaga. When the show ends, at one a.m., the crowd is on its feet, cheering, smiling, asking to take photographs. Everyone leaves happy, very happy. *Youpi!*

BEFORE I WENT to Michou's cabaret, I had never seen transvestite performances. Only their broad shoulders give these performers away as men—that, and their lack of cellulite.

I was surprised that in many of their costumes, the performers appear flat-chested, with a lean, androgynous look. The few who are given breasts (like Maria Callas in her red ball gown) are not voluptuous. And there is zero cleavage.

Then there is the testicle issue. I look hard with my journalist's trained eye and detect no telltale bulges on the bodies of performers in leotards. Not even on Cher, wearing a studded leather leotard-like costume so skimpy that her backside is covered in nothing but fishnet. The front V between her legs is so narrow I am certain something will spill out. These guys have been doing this for a long time, and just as Julie Andrews taped down her breasts while pretending to be a male transvestite nightclub star in the 1982 film *Victor Victoria*, I assume there must be a lot of creative work backstage with duct tape.

Afterward, Oscar explained how illusion is at work. "It's all in the *mousse*," he said.

"*Mousse?*" I asked.

"Yeah, like the filling of a couch."

"Ah, foam rubber!"

"Cher's torso, her butt, all of it is done in foam rubber," said Oscar. "You don't see a penis. You see nothing. When I play Chantal Ladesou, my waist, my hips, my breasts—all foam rubber!"

Michou holds forth almost every night at his table, the one closest to the bar, where he invites special guests to join him. Politics have no meaning for him. One evening, a leader of the ultra-right National Front and his much younger male companion came to sit with Michou. "I'm very, very shocked," Michou deadpanned. "I've just been told you're homos!"

He also invites guests to stop by before they sit down. He poses for pictures. He giggles a lot and likes to give the impression that he is a bit of a roué. "Don't ask me about my lovers," he told me one evening as the show was about to start. "It would fill three volumes." He loves women, he insists, from afar. "They are like flowers, very fragile," he said. "I've never touched one."

He eyed the young French male friend who had come with me. My friend is tall and lean, with smooth, fair skin, high cheekbones, and a beautiful face. "Not bad, this guy," Michou said. Just the right touch of naughtiness.

NOW ONE OF THE LAST vestiges of old Montmartre, Michou arrived here by accident. He was born to a single mother in the northern French town of Amiens in an era when premarital sex and single motherhood meant ostracism. His mother worked, so he was raised by his maternal grandmother, who couldn't read or write. Michou quit school at fourteen to do odd jobs: messenger boy, newspaper seller, stock boy, shop assistant. In 1948, at seventeen, he moved to Paris, penniless. He got a job doing chores at a restaurant before being drafted into the army; he worked in postwar Germany as a bartender in the French officers' mess. After his discharge, with financial help from an older male lover he referred to as his uncle, he became the manager of a broken-down club on the rue des Martyrs. Michou thought it resembled the waiting room in a train station. In four years, he bought the business.

His transvestite show happened by accident. For Mardi Gras in 1956, Michou, on a dare, dressed up as French sex goddess Brigitte Bardot and joined a friend onstage. "We were two *belles laides!*" he said. (The expression refers to a woman who is not beautiful—*laid* means "ugly"—but whose mystery, exoticism, or enthusiasm renders her gorgeous.) A third friend performed with them. Soon, they were joined by other "Michettes"—waiters and barmen who serve drinks and dinner before shedding their aprons and dressing up as women for the show.

"Brigitte Bardot once told me that we have the same derrière," he announced with pleasure. He pointed to a black-and-
white photo of a long-legged, long-haired, barefoot blonde in a
tutu and straw hat. The woman is looking into the camera over
her shoulder. But it is not a woman. It is Michou, about fifty years
ago, posing as Brigitte Bardot.

"I still wear the same sunglasses—but I've lost that derrière!"

In those early days, he was a pariah. "My place was considered a house of perdition," he said. "The men were prejudiced
against me. But the women came and made my reputation."
When Michou's grandmother died, he vowed that if he ever made
it big, he would honor her by helping old people. So once a month
he hosts a free lunch in his club—with wine and entertainment—
for more than eighty elderly neighborhood residents. Guest singers lead them in familiar French songs.

"In my entire life, I only loved one woman—my grandmother," he said. "I adored her. So the grandmothers and grandfathers of Montmartre are welcome here!" He slapped the table to
make his point.

For years, Michou has been a trailblazer for gay rights, a promoter of Montmartre's contemporary art scene, and a supporter
of neighborhood causes. The Republic of Montmartre, a chari-
table and cultural organization founded in 1921, has named him
its "minister of the night."

When he gave a party for Régine, the veteran Paris nightclub
and discotheque queen, at the cabaret a few years back, Bertrand
Delanoë, then the mayor of Paris, attended. When, recently,
some residents wanted to remove the children's carousel on the
place des Abbesses (too noisy, too intrusive, too tacky, they said),
he lobbied successfully to keep it there. He called it a symbol

of the chaos and whimsy of the street. "The kids in the neighborhood—they don't have the money to go to Disneyland Paris. So let them have Montmartre!"

In 2005, President Chirac decorated Michou as a *chevalier* of the Legion of Honor. "You are being decorated as the artist but also as the man with a big heart who discreetly brings such active support to great humanitarian causes," Chirac wrote in a letter that hangs on a wall of Michou's grand eighth-floor apartment in Montmartre.

"I didn't want to accept it, but everyone said, 'You must!'" he told me. Now he's so proud that every day he pins the red ribbon on the left lapel of his blue satin dinner jacket.

He calls Bernadette Chirac, the former First Lady and a fellow humanitarian, a friend. "I like her very much," he said. "She sometimes criticizes me for drinking too much champagne. One day I said to her, 'Madame, I don't touch girls; I don't touch cocaine. I don't touch hashish. Champagne keeps me young!'"

THERE WAS A TIME when the neighborhood was filled with clubs like Cabaret Michou. In the late 1800s, entertainment, alcohol, and sex mingled in Montmartre to produce a volatile brew of seediness; the lowlife included Corsican gangsters, pimps, prostitutes, vagabonds, sexual outsiders, and cardsharps. Toulouse-Lautrec, Van Gogh, and, later, Picasso and Dalí all painted scenes here. Catty-corner across the street from Cabaret Michou is the 490-seat Le Divan du Monde. When it opened as a music hall, in 1873, it was called Divan Japonais and was decorated like a Japanese brothel: silk panels on the walls, poles of bamboo, billiard tables, lacquered furniture in red and black, hostesses in kimonos. One of Toulouse-Lautrec's most famous posters shows the cancan dancer Jane Avril in profile at Divan Japonais wearing a fitted, high-necked black dress and a black bonnet that partially covers her flaming red hair.

But Le Divan du Monde has a much more important claim to fame. In the 1890s—under different ownership and name—the modern striptease is said to have been created on its stage. It featured a woman named Blanche Cavelli playing the famous cabaret artist Yvette Guilbert as she readied herself for bed. "Yvette's Going to Bed" was the name of the skit.

"When the curtain rose, a chair and a bed were onstage to represent an ordinary room," wrote Rachel Shteir in a scholarly work on the history of the striptease. "Piano music began to play, and Cavelli entered, wearing everyday clothes. She took off her gloves, her hat, and a corsage and threw them on the chair. She took off her skirt and then she removed her petticoat, her corset, her stockings, and finally her chemise, leaving her in some sort of nightgown. Finally, she climbed into bed and the lights went out." "Yvette's" undressing was so popular it inspired at least thirty similar skits in Paris.

The cabaret lived many lives, including as a comedy theater and a movie theater showing porn films. Later it was renovated—to look old and distressed—with red Chinese lanterns, a curved wrought-iron balcony, purple leopard-print drapery, and bare red light bulbs. Now it is rented out to private theater and concert organizers. There is no place to sit, so spectators stand to watch the show. I once went to hear the young American singer Ambrosia Parsley, who drank beer as she performed with a blend of enthusiasm and ennui. "I'm wearing a pretty dress on a stage in Paris," she told the crowd. "What do I have to complain about?"

Next door to Le Divan du Monde was a cabaret, now closed down, called Madame Arthur. It opened in 1948 and took its name from the song made famous by the real-life Yvette Guilbert. For a while it was more famous than Cabaret Michou. In his column in the *New York Herald Tribune*, humorist Art Buchwald once said of Madame Arthur, "It's the sort of place that makes you glad you're normal."

SPEND ENOUGH TIME with Michou, and the outer layers of frivolity peel away. He has suffered from cancer and has heart problems. He can no longer walk the hills of Montmartre on his own. He moves slowly, on the arms of others. Onstage, he occasionally forgets his lines and mangles his jokes. He no longer sings "Michou's Song," which was written in his honor, as he did every night for so many years. The only things that keep him going, he says, are champagne and his cabaret.

More and more often, when it's time for the show, the drink turns him angry. "Why are you doing this? This is all wrong!" he shouts to no one in particular. Sometimes the arguments spill out onto the street, which he knows is bad for his image.

"I'm a sad old man," Michou said one evening. He laments that Montmartre is not the same. "I knew the great moments. The fifties. There was really a soul here. There was this famous Corsican Mafia. That made the neighborhood safe. There were fruits and vegetables for every season. Small *triperies*. Now they're closed. There are all these clothing boutiques. Who needs so many clothes? Where is this neighborhood that was so lively? Where are all the artisans? The artists?

"I have the feeling that if I'm not in blue, no one will recognize me."

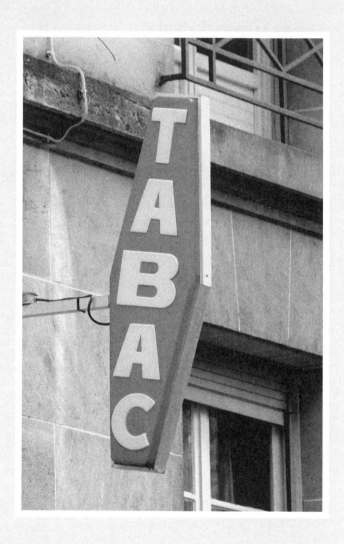

THE DIVE

...

In the room of the *bar-tabac* on the rue des Martyrs,
You can buy everything, sell everything, the best and the worst.

—2003 SONG BY THE BAND
PIGALLE ABOUT THE RUE DES MARTYRS

ONE FRIDAY CLOSE TO MIDNIGHT I FOUND MYSELF
trying to fit in at Bistrot 82. I knew I didn't. I was much older
than everyone except a lecherous drunk who looked as if he had
been glued to the same bar stool for years. But the place was so
dark I figured no one would notice me.

I was there because Cerise Sudry–Le Dû, who lives behind
Bistrot 82 at No. 82 rue des Martyrs, wanted to show me her
nighttime hangout. Cerise majored in journalism in college and
graduate school and has beaten the odds. She is a print and digital
journalist with a real job—at the free daily newspaper *Metronews*.
She is single, in her late twenties, and likes Bistrot 82 because,
unlike most Paris night spots, it does not have an entry fee. Plus,
she's already home.

"It's not really seedy here; it's not really trendy," she said
as we sat on stools at the bar that Friday night. "We're some-

where in between. There are people who are famous, people who live in the neighborhood, and people who are complete drunks."

Leila, the bartender that night, was a tall Swede with a strong build, multiple piercings, and pink hair moussed into spikes. She poured Cerise and me shots of vodka that triggered a ritual. We raised our glasses, downed our shots, and then . . .

"Watch this," said Cerise.

Leila poured a line of lighter fluid along the length of the zinc-topped bar and lit one end of it with a match. Flames rose two feet high. No one seemed flustered or shocked. Within seconds, the show was over.

"When the doors of the 82 close behind you, you enter a parallel universe," said Cerise.

If Michou's transvestite cabaret is safe, sanitized, and mostly for old-timers, Bistrot 82 is gritty, messy, and mostly for the young. It is the closest thing on the rue des Martyrs to what was once rowdy, out-of-control Montmartre.

Paris still lives on its reputation as a city of the night. Even jaded old-timers admit that it shimmers when the sun goes down and the lights go on. There is beauty to be discovered, perhaps even adventure and love. "The night suggests, it does not show," wrote Brassaï, the twentieth century's best-known photographer of Paris at night. "The night disquiets and surprises us with its otherness. It releases forces within us which by day are dominated by reason."

By day, the rue des Martyrs belongs to longtime residents, stroller-wheeling parents, curious outsiders, and shoppers of all ages. Bicyclists and motorcyclists compete with bus drivers and motorists to frustrate even the most determined pedestrians. On the lower, more gentrified end of the street, young people might linger over an iced green tea and white chocolate cookie at KB Cafeshop or a waffle at Café Marlette, known for its prepared organic muffin and pancake mixes.

By night, the tempo shifts. The night belongs to the young. The legal drinking age is eighteen, although it is easy for younger adolescents to be served. Consuming alcohol in public is allowed in France, which means drinkers overflow onto the sidewalk, especially on the Montmartre stretch. But it rarely gets out of control. Montmartre's reputation as a nighttime den of iniquity has been in a long, slow decline.

"The legend that Paris is one of the most sinful cities in the world has been passed on from generation to generation," the American humorist Art Buchwald wrote about Montmartre way back in 1952. "Unfortunately, as the tales grow stronger the sins grow weaker."

Gentrification is coming, less ferociously than at the bottom of the rue des Martyrs, but it is coming—crowding out the cheap bars, small-time drug dealers, itinerant winos, and chain-smoking streetwalkers. Even Josette, who owned this part of the rue des Martyrs as its "lady of the night" for fifty years, made enough money to retire comfortably in Nice some years ago.

Two doors down from Bistrot 82 is the Motorbass recording studio, a renovated space with state-of-the-art acoustics. Built on the site of the studio that once recorded musical legend Serge Gainsbourg (who often performed across the street), it is now the go-to place for some of the best young musicians in the world. The French band Phoenix recorded its Grammy-winning album *Wolfgang Amadeus Phoenix* here. (Thomas Mars, the lead singer of the band, is also famous for being the second husband of filmmaker Sofia Coppola and the father of their two children.) American musical artists Kanye West, Pharrell Williams, Cat Power—they've all recorded here. In 2012, the Canadian pop artist Justin Bieber recorded a song for his mother here, as a Mother's Day present.

That same year, Peoples Drugstore, which sells and serves more than five hundred brands of beer from around the world, opened down the street from Bistrot 82. It replaced a boutique that sold women's clothing. The goal of the owners is to stock one thousand brands. Cerise goes there often, to hang out and play chess. She is in an inner circle of customers invited after hours into the windowless beer and wine cave below. There, they sit on beer casks, sip wine and beer, and pass around a water pipe. "When the shop first opened, it was just a lot of old men drinking beer and playing chess," she said. "Then it was written up in the French press as the cool place to be. The clientele changed. Hipsters with mustaches came. Now you have to wait until they leave so we regulars can take back our space, and play chess as long as we like."

Peoples Drugstore is too small to accommodate many customers. But it sits on a corner with a half-block cul-de-sac that has become a meeting place for chain-smoking young beer drinkers. Even after Peoples closes, at midnight, they spread out along the curb, drink too much, and get rowdy. The residents of the apartment buildings and the clients of the small hotel in the cul-de-sac complain about the noise, but the police, who never are out in much force, see and hear little.

A bit farther south, at the intersection with the broad boulevards that form the boundary with the Ninth Arrondissement, young people sit at outdoor tables or stand on the sidewalk in front of the corner bar-bistros, keeping the street lively—and challenging for passing pedestrians.

Mohamed Maacha—his friends call him Momo—is king of this stretch of the rue des Martyrs. He opened Bistrot 82 in 1993, as an informal, no-frills neighborhood bar serving vast quantities of cheap alcohol and beer on tap and playing loud music until dawn. He describes himself as a civic-minded local businessman who watches over the street and interacts easily with the police on the rare occasions when they come to check on the place.

"With all the action we generate here, robberies on the street have stopped," he said. "The drug dealers and prostitutes have disappeared. Parents of the neighborhood feel comforted that their teenagers have a safe place to drink and party that is walking distance from home."

Momo boasts that over the years, French tennis star Jo-Wilfried Tsonga, French octogenarian singer Charles Aznavour, and Spanish filmmaker Pedro Almodóvar have visited. Bistrot 82 got another boost of celebrity in 2012 when Mika, a Lebanese-British pop singer, wrote a love song about a young woman named Karen. She sang "her dreams and ours" and other people's songs at Bistrot 82. She pledged to "make people jealous" and slept with jerks.

When Cerise celebrated her twenty-seventh birthday, her friends filled Bistrot 82 and the street outside with balloons. Because it was August, most of the neighborhood was on vacation, and Momo was delighted to host her party.

"I once did a striptease here," a waitress named Yona told Cerise.

"Oh, would you do it for me, for my birthday?" Cerise asked.

"Of course."

The DJ played Joe Cocker's "You Can Leave Your Hat On," made famous in the 1986 cult film *9½ Weeks*, in which Kim Basinger strips for Mickey Rourke.

"Yona got up on the bar, the bartender set the bar on fire, and she did a striptease," said Cerise. "This is a young woman who is really more tomboy than sex siren, not the type who would be doing a striptease, and that made it even funnier." (Unlike Basinger, Yona kept her panties on.)

"Momo shook up a bottle of champagne, so when the cork popped, the liquid shot up in the air. Everyone was dancing. It was crazy! You never know what's going to happen on the rue des Martyrs."

The two-room bar smells of sweat, stale beer, and cheap whiskey. The floor's varnish is worn, the paint on the walls yellowed and chipped, the red upholstery of a long banquette ripped to reveal its stuffing. A gleaming lighted dispenser offers six beers on tap. The rooms are decorated with oversized framed mirrors, posters of musical performances, and advertisements from magazines taped to the walls. Blinking tree lights and evergreen garlands make for a year-round Christmas feel. The tracking of bar tabs is so informal that you can slip out unnoticed without paying, or pay double because you've been stuck with someone else's bill.

One of the regulars is a thin man of indeterminate age with a thick, dark mustache. He wears a vintage French naval officer's cap and naval jacket, frumpy pants, and aviator sunglasses. He arrives drunk and sways side to side on his bar stool. He does not pose a threat because he converses mostly with himself.

"What makes this street special is not its glamour," said
Cerise. "There isn't any. But you meet really original people
here, not dangerous but very strange. And you get attached to
them."

Back home on the West Side of Buffalo, we had a word for
this kind of place: dive. A dive was a good, safe spot for us to
congregate as teenagers. Depending on the DJ, the music at
Bistrot 82 might be too loud and bass-driven for sustained conversation, too hip-hop for dancing. But when the disco-
obsessed DJ is working, you can get the best of American disco,
circa 1970s. One night he played Donna Summer's 1979
Grammy-winning "Hot Stuff," and hey, that's my generation.
Even I couldn't feel embarrassed doing my dated disco moves
on the dance floor.

Bistrot 82 used to be an all-night joint that opened at three
p.m. and closed around six a.m. But a 2008 law that banned
smoking in public places pushed smokers onto the sidewalks and
outdoor terraces. Soon the neighbors were calling the police to
complain about excessive street noise and the health hazard of
secondary smoke. They won a city order forcing Bistrot 82 to
close at two a.m.

In protest, Momo reopens on Saturday, Sunday, and Monday mornings at five a.m. for a five-hour-long *after*—or
"after-party." Sometimes on a morning jog, I hear music blar-
ing through the door and watch as the drunk and disheveled
stumble out.

"Maybe the neighbors have a point," I said to Momo one
morning.

No way, he replied. "This is Montmartre, where we party,

drink, and have fun. If all these uptight, boring people want quiet, they should never have moved to this part of town." Besides, he added, he has invested 65,000 euros in soundproofing, which should be enough evidence of his goodwill. Then his resolve dissolved into resignation. *"Ça se meurt à petit feu,"* he said of Montmartre. "It's dying a slow death."

That's debatable, at least at No. 82, where residents hold an annual celebration in the courtyard of their building. In other neighborhoods, such an event might take place with a genteel late afternoon barbecue. "Not here," said Cerise. "Here, the party starts at midnight."

At a party not too long ago, Dina, No. 82's concierge, suddenly burst into song. Although she had belonged to a musical group in her native Portugal, Dina no longer sang much. That night was different. She sang a Portuguese song of melancholy known as a *fado,* then another and another.

"No one knew she had this incredible voice," said Cerise. "People from other buildings came to their windows to listen. When she finished, everyone applauded and cheered.

"We all went to Bistrot 82, and Momo treated everyone to champagne. Then we went to another place in Pigalle and sang karaoke until dawn. Then we went to breakfast at Carlos Cheio, on the rue des Martyrs."

Momo owns not only Bistrot 82 but also a small, inexpensive restaurant called La Cave Gourmande, at No. 96, and a café and bistro—Le Bistrot des Martyrs—on the other side at No. 93. The Sacré-Coeur Basilica, at the top of Montmartre, is close by; both places appeal to tourists walking down the hill or stepping off the funicular.

"So you've become a pillar of the neighborhood," I said.

"No, not a pillar! I don't like that! I'm just an old dude."

No. 93 has an interesting history. Until a few years ago, as Chez Sorlut, it was one of Paris's most celebrated dinner clubs for what the French call *échangisme*. Clients came to dine, but they could also linger to watch or participate in sex, as this was a "libertine" place that facilitated couple swapping and group sex. "Swingers' clubs," we call them in the United States. To ensure privacy, opaque draperies covered the windows. The street in front was widened and cut into the sidewalk to designate two spaces as a delivery zone for quick drop-offs and pickups by private cars and taxis. Someone I know who visited the club told me a story about a couple he saw there: an elegant man of about seventy and a stylish, fiftyish woman wearing a mink coat. When the maître d' asked to check her coat, she handed it to him. Underneath, she was stark naked. I was amazed by the story—not that a woman was naked in a libertine club but that she was confident enough of her fifty-year-old body to show it off.

Now the club at No. 93 has become respectable, complete with Wi-Fi. Cerise uses it as a second office in which to read newspapers, conduct interviews, write stories, and meet neighbors. She ventures south of the boulevard mostly to go to and from her office—not to shop or eat or have a coffee. "I can spend the weekend without ever leaving the rue des Martyrs," she said. "It's my drug. My family was always moving when I was growing up, and I don't see my parents very often, so I have created a core of a family here. It's a good thing I have a job. Otherwise I'd let everything go and party all the time."

The next time I went to Bistrot 82, my daughter Gabriela and some of her friends came along. When I went to the bar to order drinks, a tall, handsome French man in his late twenties, his skin the color of black satin, asked if he could buy me a drink. I was gobsmacked. But I graciously declined. "Uh, thanks, but I'm here with a big group," I said.

Another young Frenchman made a similar offer. I smiled and walked away. Then a third Frenchman, also young, asked if he could kiss me.

"Kiss me?" I asked. Was he kidding? He didn't look crazy or drunk. I almost said, "I'm old enough to be your mother!" Instead, I blurted out, "I'm here with my daughter. Besides, *monsieur,* didn't you learn you must always greet people first with a *bonjour?*"

"I just wanted to kiss you!" he said, and leaned in to kiss me on both cheeks. I had to laugh. I guess this is what it's like to be a cougar.

THE
FLYING HOUSE
OF THE
VIRGIN MARY

. . .

The house of the Virgin Mary was transported to Loreto by the
"hand of angels," but not necessarily heavenly ones.

—Brochure about
Notre-Dame-de-Lorette Church

*I*T IS HEARTBREAKING THAT NOTRE-DAME-DE-LORETTE
Church is so poor and anonymous. It should be rich and famous.
It is the church where Claude Monet, Paul Gauguin, and Georges
Bizet were baptized; where the funeral mass for Théodore Géri-
cault was celebrated.

The church sits at the bottom of the rue des Martyrs and is
dedicated to Our Lady of Loreto. Growing up Catholic in Buffalo, I learned many appellations for the Virgin Mary: Our Lady
of Victory, of Lourdes, of Hope, of Perpetual Help, of the Snows,
of Guadalupe; the list goes on.

But I had never heard about Our Lady of Loreto. Her story
begins in Nazareth, in the house where Mary grew up, the very place

where the Holy Spirit told her she would become the mother of God. Toward the end of the thirteenth century, Turkish invaders threatened to destroy the house, and a band of angels decided to move it to a safer place. They scooped it up and carried it briefly to a site in what is now Croatia and eventually to the Italian hill town of Loreto.

Of course, the real story is less miraculous. In the thirteenth century, the Angeli family, a noble Italian branch of the imperial family of Constantine, thought the Muslim threat was so serious that it was time to move what was believed to have been Mary's house. So the Angelis ("the angels") dismantled it stone by stone, sailed with it across the Mediterranean Sea, and reconstructed the house in Loreto.

Ever since, Loreto has been a place of pilgrimage for Catholics. Pope John Paul II called it "the foremost shrine of international prestige devoted to the Virgin." Pope Benedict XVI made Loreto the last official visit of his pontificate, in 2012. Churches around the world have been dedicated to Our Lady of Loreto. Because her house flew, the lady inevitably became the patron saint of pilots and air travelers.

On the rue des Martyrs, however, Notre-Dame-de-Lorette has been pretty much forgotten. It originated as a chapel in 1646 but was demolished during the Terror that followed the Revolution of 1789. The current church, the first to be built in Paris after the Revolution, dates from 1836; it was designed by Louis-Hippolyte Lebas, who was soon lost to history. Alas, this was not a glorious period for French architecture.

Before I learned how the Virgin's house created the cult of Our Lady of Loreto, I thought the church might have been named after nineteenth-century female adventurers known as *lorettes*. *Lorettes*, mostly between the ages of fifteen and thirty, were beneficiaries of a general construction boom along the rue

Notre-Dame-de-Lorette. Because new buildings had damp plaster walls that took months to dry, their apartments did not appeal to upwardly mobile tenants. So the owners offered them at low prices to *lorettes*, who were required to regularly wipe the damp walls dry and to hang curtains to give the impression that the neighborhood was well-populated.

Lorettes earned their living by selling sexual favors on the streets around the church. Unlike many of the neighborhood's prostitutes, who lived controlled lives in designated houses, *lorettes* had the freedom of working as independent contractors; at first, they were portrayed as fashionable, modern, and entrepreneurial. They preferred "to take the chances of a life of complicated adventures and multiple lovers" than to lead impoverished lives, wrote Théophile Gautier, a contemporary author. Their presence, he said, gave color and unconventional style to the working-class neighborhood.

The *lorettes* were popularized in songs, plays, poetry, stories, and treatises. In his 1843 book *Filles, lorettes et courtisanes*, Alexandre Dumas marveled at the *lorettes*, who, he said, inhabited "with miraculous speed" the new Notre-Dame-de-Lorette neighborhood. He described them as "charming little beings, clean, elegant, coquettish, that one could not sort into one of the known categories. . . . It was a completely new type."

The painter Eugène Delacroix moved into a vast atelier on my street, rue Notre-Dame-de-Lorette, and the first object to strike his virtuous eyes was a "magnificent" *lorette* dressed in black satin and velvet. As she got out of a carriage, he wrote in a letter to the writer George Sand, she "let me see her leg up to her belly with the nonchalance of a goddess."

The embrace of the tight-knit neighborhood community extended even to the *lorettes*. Local merchants gave them food.

Old men paid them to lie next to them in bed, just to warm their bodies. Men of means kept them as part-time mistresses. They were even welcome at the Notre-Dame-de-Lorette Church; Paul Gavarni, the neighborhood caricaturist, drew them praying there.

They were also seen as sinister: threats to the social order and the stability of respectable society. They were demonized in literature as acquisitive social climbers who lived well by juggling multiple lovers at the same time. Dumas, for example, was as repelled as he was fascinated by the *lorette*, warning that she was as dangerous as the plague or cholera, "almost an object of terror."

In his novel *Sentimental Education*, Gustave Flaubert created the most famous—and the most complex—*lorette* in French literature: Rosanette. Flaubert loved whores and frequented them much of his adult life. He portrayed Rosanette as a ruthless opportunist who masterfully played one lover off the other. But he also made her a sympathetic figure who survived a miserable childhood, suffered the death of a child, and eventually achieved social standing by marrying—and burying—a man of wealth. She was a free spirit.

And that's how I like to think of the *lorettes*: free spirits who were named after a church.

PARIS, WITH ABOUT A HUNDRED CHURCHES, is not Rome, where the Vatican competes to dominate the landscape and every corner seems to have a church. You wander in and out of them, knowing sooner or later you'll find a treasure. Paris, by contrast, has a sophisticated, secular air.

The city has its sacred gems: the grand Notre-Dame Cathedral; Sainte-Chapelle, with more than six thousand square feet of stained glass; Saint-Julien-le-Pauvre, with its medieval facade. By comparison, Notre-Dame-de-Lorette is a poor cousin that has been allowed to deteriorate over the decades. The French state restores only national monuments, and the city of Paris prefers to invest in parish jewels like Saint-Sulpice.

It took me a while to warm up to Notre-Dame-de-Lorette. Or, rather, it took a while for the church to reveal itself to me. It has two faces. The facade, copied from an ancient Roman temple, has a pediment with sculpted figures representing faith, hope, and charity. In 1905, with secularism gaining force, the French Republic added its own touch above the entrance: a stone with the words *liberté, egalité, fraternité*.

So far, nothing special. But if you look at the church from the base of the nearby rue Laffitte, the view takes your breath away. The domes of the Sacré-Coeur Basilica, up the hill in the distance, hover over the neoclassical facade of Notre-Dame-de-Lorette. It is a magical vista of Paris—one captured over and over in photographs and postcards. I once bought a signed, framed watercolor by an unknown artist for five dollars at a yard sale in Washington, D.C. Only after I moved to Paris did I realize that it was this very scene.

The back of the church, which is the side visible from the rue des Martyrs, is dramatically different: a stone hulk without a single redeeming feature, covered with a century's worth of grime. From this perspective, it looks like a prison with a cross on top, and perhaps the ugliest church in Paris. In 2000, Paris passed a law requiring the facades of buildings to be cleaned every ten years, a practice that has brightened the physical landscape of the

city. But the law does not apply to churches, which makes the blackness of the church stand out even more.

Notre-Dame-de-Lorette can be dismissed as an example of dismal nineteenth-century church building in Paris. "Ugly, heavy, massive, sad, dirty, too," said Laurence Gillery, the restorer of antique barometers and gold-leaf frames on the other end of the rue des Martyrs. Or it can be celebrated as a miniature of Rome's Basilica di Santa Maria Maggiore, with a tall, wide nave, a double aisle, and a deep semicircular apse. There are neither vaults nor arches; there is no cross-shaped transept. "I love this church," said Bruno Racine, head of France's National Library and an expert on French art inspired by Italy. "There are wonderful paintings hidden inside; there is marvelous light. It is a little piece of Rome in Paris, a gem."

That requires a leap of faith—or at least imagination. This is not a place of floral arrangements, heady incense, or a choir of angelic voices accompanied by strings and horns. Decades of dirt—from gas lighting, candle wax, and two fires—cover most of the decorative surface in darkness.

I was sitting in the church one day with my friend Marie-Christine, who had come to pray before the lacquered wooden statue of the Virgin and infant Jesus by the nineteenth-century sculptor Carl Elshoecht. She said that if you pray to this statue, Mary will hear your prayer. Instead of looking up to heaven for divine inspiration, however, I found myself fixated on the scrolls at the top of the ionic columns lining the central aisle. They needed a good scrubbing. What a great summer project for an army of art history majors from an American university, I thought.

Then one Saturday morning I met up with Didier Chagnas, the church's caretaker and the neighborhood's self-appointed historian. He was leading a group of French out-of-towners on a tour of Notre-Dame-de-Lorette. He called himself the "keeper of the keys" and proudly carried a huge ring of church keys in his pocket. He told us that the painted decorations beneath the interior grime were considered too modern and extravagant in the mid-nineteenth century. Decades later, that judgment softened— up to a point. An 1881 book by Eugène de La Gournerie on the history of Paris and its monuments notes the church's exceptional "luxury:" "Gold, marbles, paintings, it is nothing but charm and amazement. . . . Before Notre-Dame-de-Lorette, comfort had not yet entered into holy places. . . . It looks too much like a palace, too much, if we dare, like a ballroom."

Didier also said the church was plagued from the beginning by humidity and by water flowing downhill from Montmartre. Even today, water used by early morning street cleaners ends up beneath the church. Our visit occurred shortly after completion of a major restoration of François-Édouard Picot's painting in the apse, *The Crowning of the Virgin*. It had suffered from water damage and problematic renovations, but now the robes of the Virgin and the other figures dazzle. Alas, the rest of the church looks even gloomier by contrast.

Flooding has cracked the walls, and the cracks are made worse by the vibrations of the Métro's line 12, just below. The windows along the length of the church are unadorned, translucent white blocks trimmed in dark blue—to allow in maximum light. The nave has never known the beauty of decorative stained glass.

Didier pointed to the coffered ceiling, just like Santa Maria Maggiore's. How was it that I had never noticed! Coffered wooden ceilings, with their neat geometrical forms, are typical of Italian Renaissance churches in Rome, but Notre-Dame-de-

Lorette has the only one in Paris. At first glance it looks like indented squares, rectangles, and crosses of deep blue and gold gilt. But if you look hard, you can make out the details: a dove for the Holy Spirit in the center and decorative rosettes symbolizing Mary as the "Mystical Rose."

The more Didier talked, the more animated he became, moving his body, gesticulating with his hands, and smiling. "We're in fifth-century Rome here!" he exclaimed. "This was once the most colorfully painted church in Paris!"

The tourists, eager to move on, shifted in their seats and whispered to each other. "Is he ever a talker," a boy told his mother. She giggled.

The tour guide gave Didier polite but pointed hints to wrap it up. As soon as he finished, the group rushed out the door, and I followed. Only when I was a block away did I realize Didier wasn't with us. No one in the group had thanked him, tipped him, or asked him to come along.

I returned to find him sitting alone on a bench while another group toured the church with its own guide. I apologized for having left him alone. "No problem," said Didier. Then he said that he had something to show me.

He unlocked the large wooden door of the sacristy. It swung open to reveal a small room with wood paneling and a high arched ceiling. It had the familiar smell of sacristies elsewhere, a combination of dust, wood polish, and incense. Before me was a surprise: an enormous stained-glass window, the only one in the church, showing the Virgin Mary in a red bodice, a blue skirt, and a white veil, ascending into heaven. It had been installed in the church in 1836, then destroyed when the oven of the shop on the corner exploded a century later, and painstakingly glued back together again. The riotous colors of the window were backlit with daylight.

Didier revealed other secrets: the enameled volcanic stone on a side altar; the four of the fourteen Stations of the Cross that had been stolen years before and replaced with second-rate copies; paintings covered with adhesive tape in the Chapel of Baptism in a futile effort to prevent the paint from chipping.

We climbed over a barrier onto the main altar. He showed me that some of its marble and "jewels"—the diamonds, emeralds, and rubies—were false, made of painted plaster. Then he gestured to a narrow archway and unrolled a reproduction of a painting of the four apostles. Three stood in profile; the fourth, dark circles under his eyes, stared straight ahead. Didier said the original painting was under the archway, hidden by years of dirt, candle smoke, and soot. "You can't see it—even I can't," he said. "Just know it's there."

The church's problems seem overwhelming. For the last thirty years, wooden supports have propped up two crumbling arches. Water-damaged walls continue to shed pieces of frescoes despite repairs to the roof and the gutter system. The walls of the choir have large cracks. The facade of the building needs to be repointed.

France's Observatory of Religious Heritage and SOS Paris list Notre-Dame-de-Lorette as one of the ten most threatened churches in Paris. In 2013, the World Monuments Fund, a New York–based nonprofit dedicated to preserving historic architecture and cultural heritage sites, put two Paris churches, Notre-Dame-de-Lorette and Saint-Merri, on its list of sixty-seven endangered sites around the world. Its first goal was to raise money to restore Notre-Dame-de-Lorette's cupola and the

Chapels of Marriage, Baptism, and Death. The estimate: 800,000 euros, without scaffolding, which could more than double the cost.

After taking Didier's tour, I grew more attached to the church. It is poor; it is dirty; it is neglected. But it is mine. At a time when a shortage of priests and parishioners is forcing French churches to close, Notre-Dame-de-Lorette is determined to stay open. Every morning one of its five priests celebrates Mass. Every afternoon, a priest is on duty to listen to, advise, and perhaps bless anyone who comes by. There are concerts every month, an annual Christmas sale, and activities for all ages—from catechism for children to group therapy for divorced Catholics.

One Sunday just before Christmas 2013, the church honored Didier, who was leaving his caretaking job. Father Thibault Verny called him to the altar to thank him for his work over the years. He gave Didier a one-year membership to the Louvre. Afterward, parishioners crowded around to congratulate him. We walked together to the church's auxiliary building, a few blocks away, for a reception in his honor.

Then Didier and I were alone. "You know what's going on?" he asked. "You know that this Mass was my good-bye?"

"But you still have the keys, don't you?"

"No. I had to give them back."

SOMETIME LATER, AS A GUEST at an artists and writers retreat in Umbria, I learned that the hill town of Loreto—the site of the Virgin Mary's flying house, the inspiration for my Notre-Dame-de-Lorette Church—was only a hundred miles away. I had to go.

I arrived to find a sixteenth-century domed basilica with soaring ceilings and two dozen chapels. It made Notre-Dame-de-Lorette seem pitiful by contrast. At the center of the basilica stands a huge, lavishly carved marble structure designed by Donato Bramante, the Italian Renaissance architect. Each of the four sides tells a story: the birth of Mary; the Annunciation by the angel Gabriel; the birth of Jesus; and, by far the most dramatic scene, angels carrying off Mary's house. Inside Bramante's structure is the "house" itself.

The house has one room and measures about twenty-eight feet by thirteen. Local Italian brick sits atop a base of stones from Nazareth. An elaborate altar of colored marble and gold gilt, added later, holds a statue of Mary and the infant Jesus. A nearby museum exhibits dozens of artworks—paintings, sculptures, ceramics, and tapestries of varying quality and spanning several centuries—that depict Mary's house in midair.

I expected the site to be saturated with tourists. Luckily, I had just missed a delegation of thousands of young people who had walked through the night on an annual pilgrimage from the nearby town of Macerata. They had been thrilled to get a phone call of encouragement from Pope Francis; he told them life was made for doing "great things" and asked them to pray for him. (The museum includes a special bedroom reserved for the pope, should he come to visit.) In the gift shop, I loaded up with Madonna of Loreto postcards, holy cards, medals, devotional prayer books, and statuettes to take home to friends on the rue des Martyrs.

I resisted the temptation to buy Madonna of Loreto snow globes.

A STREET FIT
FOR A POPE

...

Is it true, great Father, that the story is told somewhere in the
Lives of the Saints of a holy saint martyred for his faith who,
when his head was cut off at last, stood up, picked up his head,
and, "courteously kissing it," walked a long way, carrying it in
his hands. Is that true or not, honored Father?

—FYODOR DOSTOYEVSKY, *The Brothers Karamazov*

Your Holiness, it will be a miracle if my letter reaches you.
But miracles happen, no?

—MY LETTER TO POPE FRANCIS INVITING HIM
TO THE RUE DES MARTYRS

ONE DAY, POPE FRANCIS WILL COME TO PARIS. AND WHEN
he does, he will have to visit the rue des Martyrs. There is a small
crypt under a defunct chapel that he will want to see.

The crypt is just off the top of the rue des Martyrs at No. 11
rue Yvonne-le-Tac, named after a female leader of the French
Resistance. Called the Martyrium, the crypt is thought to be the
site of the beheading of Saint Denis and his two companions.

Before surrendering to death, the legend goes, Denis carried his head several miles to the north. And that's the site that has been celebrated over the centuries. There, in what is now the Paris suburb of Saint-Denis, the showpiece Saint-Denis Basilica was built. Considered the first Gothic church, it is a medieval flight of fancy and a symbol of religious excess, with glorious stained-glass windows and hundreds of figures carved into the stone facade. All the kings and queens of France from the tenth to the eighteenth centuries were buried there. Meanwhile, the Martyrium, where Denis was decapitated, has little star appeal. If Saint Geneviève, the patron saint of Paris, who saved the city from Attila the Hun in the fifth century, had not lobbied for a chapel here, the site might have been forgotten.

I haven't found evidence that Pope Francis has a particular devotion to Saint Denis. But he is a Jesuit—the first Jesuit to become pope. The Martyrium is the place where Ignatius Loyola and his compatriots took their vows before he created the Society of Jesus, better known as the Jesuits. Besides, France is often referred to as the "eldest daughter of the church" because of its unbroken religious union with Rome since early Christianity. Pope Francis could put the crypt on the map. After I learned about the Martyrium, I decided that I needed to invite him to the rue des Martyrs.

Here is the backstory of the Jesuits and the Martyrium: Ignatius Loyola was born in 1491 to a rich and noble Basque family. But he was less a nobleman than a street fighter, gambler, and ladies' man. He was rumored to have fathered a child out of wedlock. "Until the age of twenty-six, he was a man given over to the vanities of the world," Ignatius said in his autobiography, which he wrote in the third person.

As an officer in the Spanish army fighting the French, Ignatius was seriously wounded in battle. After enduring many painful operations, he spent his convalescence reading the only books available: stories about Jesus and the saints. Powerfully moved by the stories, Ignatius put down his sword to become a religious pilgrim. He confessed his sins and threw himself on God's mercy. He experienced dramatic mood swings, one day thinking about suicide, the next day reveling in mystical union with God. He prayed, fasted, begged, and flagellated himself. He let his hair and fingernails grow. He eventually found peace in giving up those practices.

He moved to Paris in 1528 to further his religious education, learn Latin, and earn a master of arts degree. He also banded together with six other young men, who became his closest companions. Together, they pledged to separate themselves from the world, to follow Jesus in poverty and chastity, and to go to Jerusalem to convert Muslim Turks. If they could not make it to Jerusalem, they would go to Rome to meet the pope and do whatever they could to promote "the greater glory of God and the good of souls," Ignatius wrote.

They decided to take their vows in the chapel attached to the Martyrium, perhaps because of its location: well outside the Paris city limits at that time and hidden from spies of the Inquisition, who were eager to uncover any deviation from a strict interpretation of Catholicism. In 1534, on the feast day of the Assumption of the Virgin Mary into heaven, the men walked up the path that would become the rue des Martyrs.

Pierre Favre, a Frenchman and one of Ignatius Loyola's band of six, had been ordained a priest only a few weeks before. He celebrated Mass for the group, and one after another they proclaimed their vows. A nun in the adjoining convent was so moved by what she witnessed that she gave the men keys to the chapel. "Hindsight surely allows us to see in the event of that August day the cornerstone of the future Society of Jesus," wrote Reverend John W. O'Malley, a Jesuit scholar. Six years later, the pope approved the creation of the Jesuit order.

Since then, the Martyrium has had its ups and downs. It was badly damaged during the siege of Paris in 1590, and some of the nuns living in the abbey were said to have resorted to prostitution to support themselves.

Workers rebuilding the crypt in 1611 discovered a mysterious stone vault. A few letters carved into it were still legible: mar . . . clemin . . . dio . . . "Mar" stood for martyr; "Clemin," for Pope Clement, who was believed to have sent Saint Denis to Paris; and "Dio" for Dionysius, the Greek name for Denis, or so it was thought. The discovery led to furious speculation that Saint Denis was buried there, not at the site of the Saint-Denis Basilica. The Martyrium became a necessary destination for pilgrims in Paris.

The devotional frenzy ended with the French Revolution, which banned pilgrimages and monastic orders and ordered the sale of religious houses. During the Terror that followed, the chapel bells were melted down, the statues destroyed, the paintings and other art objects stolen or sold. The abbey became a military barracks, the crypt a toolshed. The crypt was restored, along with an adjoining chapel, in the 1880s. But it never again had star status. In 1982 the city of Paris expropriated and secularized the site. It removed the stained glass from the chapel, which it then turned into a cafeteria for a middle school.

Most Paris guidebooks ignore the crypt. There is no Saint Denis tourist shop or café, no Ignatius Loyola bookstore or tapas bar across the street. It has no outstanding architectural details or works of art. The crypt is open to the public for only three hours a week, on Friday afternoons, plus once a month on weekends. For years there was not even an official plaque describing the site's significance. No one stands at the door to greet passersby.

The few visitors are either curious tourists or devout pilgrims, like the four Japanese who arrived after the tsunami struck their homeland in March 2011. They prayed; they wept; they banged their heads on the stone floor in a sign of subjugation, sacrifice, and self-flagellation.

The caretaker is not a priest or a nun but a Polish-born actor and theater producer named Zygmunt Blazynsky. He has long, thinning hair and the sort of shabby look that used to be described as bohemian. He has worked as a volunteer here for more than two decades, because he believes the crypt is the most mystical and important spiritual site in Paris. He also appreciates its superior acoustics and uses it to host concerts, plays, and literary readings.

The crypt is stark in its simplicity. It is furnished with a few rows of wooden pews made only slightly more comfortable with cushions. The stone altar is unadorned. The most precious objects are a medieval stone bas-relief of the martyrdom of Saint Denis and a nineteenth-century painting of Ignatius and his followers taking their vows.

I was most fascinated by a large reproduction that showed Saint Denis as a "head carrier," or *céphalophore*. In traditional stories of the saints, there are well over a hundred martyrs who carried their heads. They are difficult to portray in art because there's no accepted way to depict their halos. Above the neck? Or on the severed head?

The crypt celebrates four Masses a year. Even on October 9— the feast day for Saint Denis—only about twenty people arrived for the Mass I attended, and five belonged to the choir. The others seemed to be regulars, ranging in age from sixty to eighty or so. Four visiting Jesuits were honored guests.

Father P. Jean Laverton, the rector of Sacré-Coeur, up the Montmartre hill, did his best to liven things up. "There is not much to see in this chapel, but symbolically, this is a holy place of Christian prayer!" he exclaimed. "Saint Denis was martyred on this hill. Throughout the centuries, the people of Paris and the great saints of the church have come to pray here. With them, we are in the great communion of saints of the church!"

One day, Zygmunt introduced me to Éric de Langsdorff, vice-president of the volunteer association devoted to preserving and promoting the crypt, and Sister Chantal de Seyssel, who had once lived in what had been the convent next door.

I asked if I could become a member.

"If you don't make a revolution, sure!" said Éric. Everyone thought that was very funny.

"And it's not expensive!" exclaimed Zygmunt. "Ten euros!"

"We're not very gifted with money," said Éric.

Zygmunt then had something to show me. We walked up the stairs and out the door, where he pointed to a white marble plaque on the outer wall of the crypt. The Martyrium's tiny volunteer association had raised 1,800 euros to have it done. It had been installed a few weeks before.

"Visitor," it says in French, "Here, in the 5th century A.D., Saint Geneviève erected a chapel dedicated to Saint Denis, the first bishop of Paris, martyred in the 3rd century with Saint Rusticus and Saint Eleutherius. It is also here that on August 15, 1534, Saint Ignatius of Loyola and his companions made the vow of Montmartre that committed them to the service of the Church and led, six years later, to the approval by Pope Paul III of the Order of the Jesuits: the Society of Jesus. The Crypt, restored in the late 19th century, perpetuates the memory of these two events."

That's when I told Zygmunt and Éric about my plan to invite the pope to the rue des Martyrs. They embraced the idea and immediately fell into a discussion of protocol. Zygmunt wondered whether Francis retained his Jesuit identity as pope, and if so, would have to ask the Jesuits for permission. Éric was sure that Francis no longer had to obey the Jesuit order even though he kept his Jesuit vows. They debated whether the attachment to the Jesuits was real or merely sentimental. Éric insisted that the pope could make only a private visit, nothing official.

"Fine with me!" I said. "Private, public, official, nonofficial. He has to come here!"

Then I broke into English and said, "Yes, we can!"

Everyone laughed.

"We're crazy," I said. "But good crazy. You have to be a little crazy in life. Saint Ignatius was crazy when he came here with his friends to make their crazy promises to God."

We all agreed. And with that, we parted, promising to meet again soon.

ON DECEMBER 17, 2013, Pope Francis's seventy-seventh birthday, we had a sign. The pope canonized Pierre Favre—the

French priest who had celebrated Mass at the crypt when Ignatius and his friends took their vows. In 1872, Favre had been "beatified," or declared a "Blessed" of the church, the first step in the process, but until then he had not attained sainthood.

Favre's canonization was a bold move because Francis did not follow usual Vatican protocol. A candidate for sainthood is supposed to have performed two miracles. As far as anyone knew, Favre had not. So Francis resorted to "equivalent canonization," used by popes on rare occasions to bestow sainthood on a candidate who died long ago and whom the Catholic Church reveres as holy. It's done without much fanfare or a formal canonization ceremony.

It turns out that Francis has a special devotion to Favre, which he explained during an August 2013 interview with the Jesuit priest Antonio Spadaro in *La Civiltà Cattolica*, the Italian Jesuit journal. Francis said that he had been inspired by Favre's "dialogue with all, even the most remote and even with his opponents; his simple piety, a certain naïveté perhaps, his being available straightaway, his careful interior discernment, the fact that he was a man capable of great and strong decisions but also capable of being so gentle and loving."

Pierre Favre, Spadaro concluded, is Francis's "favorite Jesuit."

In January 2014, Francis celebrated Mass to mark Favre's canonization in the Chiesa del Gesù in Rome, the Jesuits' most important church. Both Favre and Saint Ignatius are buried there. In his homily, Pope Francis praised "Saint Peter" (as Favre is now known in English), for his desire to "empty himself" and allow Christ to fill his heart and life.

Good grief, I thought. *If I still lived in Rome, I could have been there!* The Chiesa del Gesù is just across the street from the Palazzo Altieri, the seventeenth-century building where I lived for nearly three years in the early 1980s, as Rome bureau chief for *Newsweek*. The Chiesa del Gesù had been my church. I took visitors there to see Ignatius's over-the-top marble-and-bronze tomb. It is framed by columns encrusted with lapis lazuli; the globe above representing the Trinity is the largest piece of lapis lazuli in the world. A sculpture on one side represents faith defeating idolatry; one on the other, religion lashing heresy. Very Jesuit. And very different from the poor, plain crypt in Paris.

IT WAS TIME TO WRITE Pope Francis a letter. I had enough going for me to sound respectable. I had been an undergraduate at Canisius College, a Jesuit college in my hometown of Buffalo. My father had earned his degree at Canisius during the Depression. While based in Rome for *Newsweek*, I covered the Vatican and traveled with the pope. I have a black-and-white photo of me chatting with Pope John Paul II on a plane during one of his foreign trips. Best of all: my middle name is Frances.

I sought guidance from family, friends, and sources.

My younger daughter, Gabriela, thought Nick Darre, an Argentine friend from high school in Paris, had a family connection. Gabby texted him in Buenos Aires.

Gabby: Random but who is it in ur fam knows the pope again lol?

Nick: My cousin's maternal grandmother.

Gabby: Nice! My mom wants to write to him haha.

Nick: I'll see what I can do. I can't guarantee anything. . . . I'll give you his cell number.

Gabby: Lol

Nick: They used to talk all the time and meet up quite often.

Gabby: That's awesome.

Nick tried to put his cousin's grandmother on the case. But she was getting old and seemed confused when he called to explain our mission. Not long before, she had written her own letter to Francis, requesting human, not divine, intervention. One of her grandsons had been expelled from school, and she'd asked Francis to use his influence to get him accepted into another one. Although Francis hadn't replied, he'd had a good excuse: he was becoming pope.

We assumed he had changed his cell phone number, so I cast a wider net. The Jesuit priest Tom Reese, senior analyst for the *National Catholic Reporter,* is one of the best-informed outsiders on the Vatican. He wrote me an e-mail: "Great idea, but you will get nowhere without the support of the local archbishop and French Jesuits."

Bruno Racine, head of France's National Library, has superb contacts from his days as head of the Villa Medici in Rome. He told me to put my cell phone number in my letter, because the pope has been known to simply pick up the phone and call people who reach out to him.

Elisabetta Povoledo, a friend and a correspondent in the Rome bureau of the *New York Times,* sent me the pope's personal address:

"P.O. One, Vatican City."

Naturally.

I told my husband, Andy, about my plan at breakfast the

next morning. When I mentioned the pope's address, he looked up from his newspaper and asked, "Is this like writing to Santa Claus?"

Hah! I'd show him.

I REACHED OUT TO PHILIP PULLELLA, an American journalist I knew from my days in Rome, who covers the Vatican for Reuters. Thirty-odd years ago I had hired his wife, Marilena, as my administrative assistant in Rome. "Go for it," he wrote. "He responds to the weirdest of people, so why not you?"

He said my letter "should be a mix of respect and enthusiasm. It should not cloud your own personality and passion about the street/crypt. And of course mention that you are a Jesuit-educated American who has conquered the world, stared down dictators, etc., etc., but finds so much true bliss on that little rue with the little crypt that you are writing an entire book about it."

I knew that "Dear Holy Father" wasn't quite right.

Phil advised addressing the pope as "Your Holiness."

He said I should mention that my Jewish husband and I were married by a rabbi and a priest—and not just any priest but a Jesuit, the late Reverend Vincent O'Keefe, who had been vicar general of the Jesuits and general assistant to Reverend Pedro Arrupe when he headed the Jesuit order. Phil said that when the pope was archbishop of Buenos Aires, he had developed a close friendship with Abraham Skorka, an Argentine rabbi. The pair co-hosted a televised Bible discussion, coauthored a book of lively theological conversations, and continued to talk via e-mail about Jewish-Catholic relations.

I addressed my letter to "Your Holiness" and began like this:

"It will be a miracle if my letter reaches you. But miracles happen, no? I am confident that during your papacy, Your Holiness, you will come to France, 'the eldest daughter of the Church.' So I am asking you to consider a visit to a very special but forgotten place in Paris: the crypt and chapel that mark the place where Saint Denis and his two companions were martyred. As you know, it was also in the crypt and chapel that on the feast of the Assumption in 1534, Saint Ignatius Loyola and six companions took their first vows of poverty and chastity."

I evoked God's presence on the rue des Martyrs: "Saint Ignatius told his missionaries to write not only about their spiritual ministries but also about the reality of everyday life—'anything that seems extraordinary.' The rue des Martyrs and the tiny crypt and chapel are extraordinary. Ignatius's motto was 'finding God in all things,' and it is not difficult to find God on the rue des Martyrs."

I ended by saying, "Perhaps, Your Holiness, you will one day walk on the same route walked by Saint Denis and Saint Ignatius and arrive at the Saint Denis crypt. I will be there— with all the residents, merchants, workers, and students of the rue des Martyrs—to cheer you on. . . . I hope at the very least, Your Holiness, that my letter has brought a smile to your face."

To help me reach the pope, I called the office of the Holy See in Paris and asked to meet Luigi Ventura, the papal nuncio. His assistant said I should make my request in a letter sent through the post office. Neither an e-mail nor a scanned letter via e-mail would do. So I sent a letter and about ten days later received a reply from Ventura. He rejected my project in brutally cold diplomatese.

"Allow me to tell you that I am not competent in that which

interests you," he wrote in French. "I do not see what I could bring to you by meeting you."

I got the message. I was on my own.

I sent Phil my letter to the pope in French and Spanish. Marilena translated it into Italian. Now what? "We're at a crossroads," Phil said. "The pope gets so much mail that the tiny office that deals with it is swamped."

Phil had written a story for Reuters disclosing that the office receives about 6,000 letters a week, more than 300,000 a year. Monsignor Giuliano Gallorini, head of the office that handles letters to the pope, leads a team of one nun and two laywomen, who work in one small room. They sort the letters by language. Monsignor Gallorini told Vatican Television that most of the letters are about "difficulties," mostly illness but also economic distress. "They ask for prayers," he said.

More urgent and personal letters go to the pope's two private priest secretaries. "These are the ones that are a little more delicate, that have to do with questions of conscience," Gallorini said.

My letter fit neither of the categories.

I apologized to Phil for involving him.

"No, no, there's no reason why Francis won't say he'll come to your street one day," he said. "Your letter is so cute, so innocent, so sincere."

So naïve?

Phil plunged me into a convoluted world of Vatican politics and protocol that I hadn't dealt with in thirty years. He ran through possible scenarios.

First, the slam dunk: Phil would give my letter to the pope himself the next time he was in the "pool"—that is, when he was one of the few journalists chosen to cover a papal event, who then "pools" the information to the rest of the press corps. That, we decided, would be too brazen.

Second, the Swiss Guard: Phil would give the letter to the commandant of the Pontifical Swiss Guard, which protects the Vatican.

"You mean just go up to the Vatican front gate and hand it to one of the guards on duty outside?" I asked.

"Not any Swiss Guard," said Phil. "The commandant. I could ask him for guidance."

That, we agreed, was too uncertain.

Third, the payback: "There is a Jesuit who owes me a favor," he said.

Sounded good to me.

So Phil took the letter to Father Spadaro, the Jesuit priest who had interviewed the pope for *La Civiltà Cattolica*. Father Spadaro was amused. He smiled and read parts of the letter aloud. He told Phil he had once visited the Martyrium off the rue des Martyrs. He said he saw the pope regularly and that he'd be happy to help. He hand-delivered my letter to the pope's office in Santa Marta, the Vatican guesthouse where he has taken up residence.

I prepared for a phone call from the Vatican. I rigged up a speaker system on the dining room table. I readied a recording device to preserve the conversation and capture every one of the pope's words. I wrote a script in Italian.

"What's with the speakers and wires?" Andy asked me a few days later.

I told him I was waiting for Pope Francis to call.

"You're joking, right?" he said.

So far, Pope Francis hasn't called. He hasn't written.

But I refuse to give up.

Like Ignatius Loyola, Francis exhorts us to find God in all things. "I look forward to the surprise of every day," he once wrote.

Me, too.

LE KALE AMÉRICAIN
EST ARRIVÉ!

. . .

And here and there gleamed the glistening ruddy brown
of a hamper of onions, the blood-red crimson of a heap of
tomatoes, the quiet yellow of a display of squash and the
somber violet of the aubergine; while numerous fat black
radishes still left patches of gloom amidst the quivering
brilliance of the general awakening.

—ÉMILE ZOLA, *The Belly of Paris*

I LEFT TOWN ONE AUGUST, AND WHEN I RETURNED IN
September, Ali Belkessa and Fahmi Hamrouni, the greengrocers
between the hardware and cheese stores at the bottom of the
street, had disappeared.

Andy detected the first sign of something amiss.

"There's a new team at Ali's shop," he told me.

"They must still be on vacation," I said.

When I went shopping for fruit and vegetables, I asked about
Ali and Fahmi.

"They're gone," said the man in charge.

He told me his name was Kamel Ben Salem. He said he and

his father-in-law Abdelhamid Ben Dhaou bought the shop from Ali in June and spent the month of August renovating. They had been open for four days.

"Where did they go?" I asked.

"To the Seventeenth, I think," he said, meaning an arrondissement to the northwest.

I wanted the address; Kamel said he didn't have it.

How could this be? Ali belonged on the rue des Martyrs. A big man with a big belly, he knew me by my first name and kissed me on both cheeks whenever I stopped by. When he became a father, the street knew and rejoiced.

Ali's shop cascaded gloriously onto the street most Sunday mornings, when the rue des Martyrs was closed to traffic. He set up tables with bargains of the week and loudly hawked his goods, the only merchant to do so. Some people delighted in his effusive spirit; others heard his shouts about three cartons of strawberries for the price of two and thought he belonged in an Algerian souk, not a gentrifying neighborhood of Paris. Ali had been born in Algeria, while most of the street's greengrocers came from the Tunisian island of Djerba, some from the same extended family. To them, Ali was an outsider.

I'm a reporter. How had I not known that Ali and Fahmi were leaving?

Ali had promised to take me to buy produce at the vast Rungis wholesale market; Fahmi had once featured in a broadcast I did for NBC's *Today Show*, about an official campaign to coax Parisians to be nicer to tourists. He was filmed telling me about carrots. Just about every time I saw him, I joked that in America, he was a star! I thought we had a relationship.

So why didn't they tell me?

I crossed the street to the café at No. 8, where Ali and Fahmi had alternated taking their breaks every morning. Mahmoud Allili, the owner, is also from Algeria; he and Ali had been close. Mahmoud shrugged. "Everybody knew they were leaving."

"But we should have had a party for them!" I said. "We should have taken photos."

He shrugged again. Such sentimentality had nothing to do with business.

I went next door and asked Valérie Levin, the baker's wife, if she had heard. "Sure," she replied. "We knew they were moving. But you don't talk much about these things."

I walked to the more upscale fruit and vegetable shop up the street then owned by Ezzidine Ben Abdollah. Even though Ali had been competition, the two men had liked and respected each other. "He got a great offer," said Ezzidine. "I assumed you knew."

He said Ali had gone to work as a wholesale buyer at Rungis for his uncle, who owned several greengrocery shops in Paris. "You make more money doing that than what we do here on the rue des Martyrs," he explained.

Like Ezzidine, the new owner was from Djerba, but Ezzidine told me that he missed Ali. "He knew everyone's name," he said. "He came by just to talk—about produce, about business, about our families."

I stopped last at the cheese shop next to Ali's. Annick Chataigner said she had known in the spring that Ali had plans to sell. "I tried to persuade him to stay. I told him he belonged here. I told him I felt I was losing a son!"

And that was that. Everyone had known. Except me. I thought about why and came up with two reasons. First, France is a country of secrets. Keeping them, and deciding when to trade in them, is more than a game; it's a national survival strategy. Ugly truths might disturb the surface calm. What harm comes from disguising them if it preserves a pleasant outer world?

Second, the rue des Martyrs is a village, with insiders and outsiders. The insiders, in this case, were the merchants. Next came the people who lived on the street. Then came everyone else. As a newcomer and a foreigner, I was everyone else.

I was reminded of something my paternal Sicilian grandfather, Tom Sciolino, taught me as a child. He cursed the *stranieri,* the "foreigners." In reality, the *stranieri* were the outsiders, the ones who could not be trusted. My grandfather saw the world as concentric circles with himself as the center, then the family, then people who had emigrated from his hometown, then Sicilians, then other Italians, then everyone else. Anyone in authority was to be avoided. The rules of the rue des Martyrs are not quite as stark. But there is some truth in the *stranieri* theory.

Gradually, I got over Ali and Fahmi's leaving and decided to give the new guys a chance. Kamel boasted that he had added shelves to stock more merchandise. He had installed bright fluorescent lighting and two Formica-topped tables for the scales and cash boxes. He raved about his produce.

"My father-in-law has been in the business for forty years," said Kamel. "We have the best sources at Rungis."

"What is really good today?" I asked.

"Mirabelles!" he said, pointing to a box piled high with deep-yellow plums.

"Mirabelles! They are terrible this summer."

Kamel handed me one. "Taste it," he commanded. "It's *top.*"

Top? Oh my! English was invading the rue des Martyrs.

I popped the small plum whole into my mouth. The skin was firm but not tough. The flesh was soft, the liquid sweet. Kamel was right. The mirabelle was *top*.

"I'll take a kilo," I said.

The next test: arugula. Ali and Fahmi had never had good arugula. Theirs was packaged in plastic and belonged in a supermarket, not a greengrocery. Kamel lifted a translucent sheet from a box to reveal crisp baby arugula. His look said, "I told you."

I saw him from a new perspective. And then I thought I recognized him. Of course. He had been the greengrocer on the upper rue des Martyrs. For eight years. He belonged. Abdelhamid told me that his father and Fahmi's grandfather were brothers. He had known Fahmi since he was born.

Day after day, Abdelhamid and Kamel charmed me. Every morning before dawn, Abdelhamid drove to Rungis to choose the produce himself. He showed an artistic side as he arranged peaches in pyramids and mixed tomatoes of many colors and sizes in one bin. He lined the bins with lime-green paper to bring out the natural colors of the produce. He introduced new items, like sweet corn. Corn! The French feed it to animals. The only place I had ever found sweet corn in the neighborhood was at the Picard supermarket, husked, wrapped in plastic, and frozen. Kamel and Abdelhamid use paper bags, not plastic ones like the supermarket does, to keep leafy vegetables from being crushed. The bags are not like the plain ones found in America. These are made in France of recycled paper—biodegradable, resistant to humidity, and decorated with an illustration of a cart overflowing with colorful fruits and vegetables.

We bonded. When I needed a centerpiece one Thanksgiving, Abdelhamid and Kamel offered me a twenty-pound gourd. It resembled a squat tan pumpkin with voluptuous curves. It cost twenty-eight euros.

"But I only need it for one night," I said.

Kamel had an elegant solution: he lent it to me. Not only that, he carried it to my apartment and put it at the center of the table. I returned it the next day.

One day I walked in vowing to buy only a head of lettuce, two avocados, and four apples. Nothing more. As I left, I spotted a box of fresh artichoke bottoms. Kamel had painstakingly cut away the outer leaves, leaving only the smallest ones to keep the flesh from turning brown. The flesh should not be exposed until just before cooking.

"I'll give you a great price!" he said.

"I don't need artichoke bottoms!"

"Ten euros!"

"That's too expensive!"

He picked up a whole artichoke the size of a grapefruit and threw it on the scale.

"One artichoke is six euros!" he said. "I'm giving you such a deal. And all the work I did comes free."

I couldn't resist. But I left in protest. "You're too good a merchant, Kamel," I said. "I'm going to stop passing by your shop every day."

After that, I began calling him the most seductive grocer in Paris. Over time, I learned that the two grocers relished gustatory challenges. So I gave them a big one: to find *chou frisé non pommé*, a.k.a. kale.

The French do not know from kale. To them it is cabbage, pure and simple. And cabbage is a reminder of the dietary deprivation of World War II, when boiled cabbage became an unpleasant fixture of the dinner table. The French cannot even agree on what to call kale, which has at least five names. The technical term, *chou frisé non pommé*, translates unappetizingly as "curly headless cabbage."

I discovered kale in Paris thanks to a young American crusader for crucifers, Kristen Beddard, who brought it to the city's food markets. The Joan of Arc of kale, she created the Kale Project, reporting kale sightings and pitching kale to chefs and vegetable farmers. She gave me some of her precious kale seeds. I put them in a pot on my kitchen windowsill and dutifully watered it every other day. After two months, I had a healthy plant, four inches tall, with several curly leaves. I took it to Kamel and Abdelhamid. I explained that the ancient Greeks and Romans had cultivated kale-like primitive cabbages. I said that because kale grows well in cold climates, it caught on big in Germany, the Netherlands, and England. I said it is a "superfood" in the United States, that Barack Obama and his family eat it, and that every respectable New York restaurant offers at least one kale dish on its menu.

They were intrigued. Abdelhamid built a little shrine with fresh lychees and put my kale plant on top. In black marker, he wrote on the clay pot, *"Chou américain:* Kale." Tourists took photos. Abdelhamid promised to look for it at the Rungis market. A week later, he reported that not a single vegetable distributor carried kale.

Then, one day, *le kale est arrivé!*

Kamel was so excited that he chased after me up the rue des Martyrs, brandishing a big bunch of the curly green. He had six of them. I bought them all.

THE
RESURRECTION
OF FISH

· · ·

Paris is a gray and rainy city, but when spring arrives and
the terraces fill and street singers seem to emerge from every
corner singing La Vie en Rose, the city turns into the best
place in the world to be happy.

—ENRIQUE VILA-MATAS,
Never Any End to Paris

*I*N HIS SEARCH FOR A NEW FISHMONGER AT NO. 5,
Mayor Jacques Bravo visited the National Union of the French
Fish Trade and pleaded with its representatives to find someone,
anyone, who knew fish. A young couple, perhaps, whose family
had been in the business?

Some mornings Bravo arrived by five a.m. at the vast fresh
fish hall of the Rungis wholesale food market, dressed in a suit,
the red rosette proclaiming him an *officier* of the Legion of Honor
in his lapel. He wandered up and down the aisles, shivering in the
refrigerated space, as he lobbied fishmongers to take a chance on
the rue des Martyrs.

In time, a small fish-store chain assumed the lease on the shop Marc Briolay had given up. Over several months, the new owner gutted and rebuilt the space, installing new shelves, lighting, and a state-of-the-art system to automatically spray ice-cold mist on the fish from vents mounted on the ceiling. He hired more fishmongers than before and bought a large lobster tank and, *bien sûr*, a new ice machine. The shop opened without fanfare—but with a lot of gorgeous fish. Counters piled high with oysters, mussels, and clams on beds of algae spilled onto the sidewalk; a counter in the back held cooked lobsters, crabs, and several varieties of shrimp. Behind that were the fishmongers' stations for washing, scale scraping, filleting, and gutting.

A new fishmonger, also named Marc, arrived: big, bearded, with only one tooth visible when he smiled. He was a man who loved fish. He gushed over *coq rouge*, a small, reddish-orange, polka-dotted fish from Senegal.

"They are so beautiful!" he said. "Imagine grilling them whole."

He preferred the ugly ones, the uglier the better. He held up a *lotte*—a monkfish. It had long filaments sprouting from its head and the wide grin and beady eyes of a sea monster. "I use it in bouillabaisse," he said. "If I bake it with a dash of pastis, I'm in Marseille!"

Joël Vicogne, the son of the landlord, joined the new team. His colleagues in the old fish shop had regarded him with suspicion, but his new ones treated him as a trusted veteran, and this acknowledgment of his status gave him confidence. He continued to cut impossibly thin slices of smoked salmon. But he took on new responsibilities: twice a week he prepared *brandade de morue*—a puree of salt cod with potatoes, olive oil, and garlic—

and supervised a new display of prepared foods: octopus and shrimp made half a dozen ways and an assortment of *taramas*.

Joël had not been particularly friendly to me when the Briolays ran the place. He knew where my loyalties lay. But soon he and his colleagues began to warm up; Joël even greeted me with kisses on both cheeks. And he winked! Now when I want tuna filets, the fishmongers don't wrap the pieces already on display; instead, they cut fresh ones from fish stored in the back room, especially for me. When I need a whole salmon for a party, they bend the rules and custom-cook it. During scallop season, they scoop the scallops fresh from their shells.

Justine Briolay, the daughter of the shop's former owner, did not follow her parents to the countryside. She lived nearby and had made a life for herself on the rue des Martyrs. She went to work for the butcher two doors down from the fish store, in the part of the shop that served terrines and charcuterie. She learned how to differentiate the terrines, oversee and weigh the prepared salads, and slice the cold cuts. The counter on the other side is for serious butchery, a man's job. Of the forty thousand butchers in France, only a few hundred are women.

Change continued on the rue des Martyrs as new businesses replaced the old. While some stalwarts survived, others did not. It was as if a Kansas tornado had ripped through, sparing certain targets, destroying others. A newspaper and magazine shop halfway up the rue des Martyrs went out of business, but the owner moved into a space on the street where I live. I decided to support him by canceling many of my home delivery subscriptions and stopping in frequently to buy his magazines.

The rue des Martyrs had once been famous for shops run by private laundresses; most closed their doors decades ago, when residents began buying washing machines. The last custom laundry and dry cleaner closed in 2010, and more than two years later, an outlet of the Belgian chain Le Pain Quotidien moved into its space. On opening day, I was the first customer, a newcomer welcoming a newer-comer.

A few days later I went to Le Pain Quotidien with Margherita Frezza, a young Italian architect who lives with her French boyfriend across the street. I wanted to see the restaurant through her eyes. She hated it. "In real cafés and bistros, the menus are handwritten on blackboards in white script every day," she said. "Here, the script is phony—it's in permanent white ink. Yes, the scales are old, but they're exactly like the ones in just about every other Pain Quotidien."

She tapped the picture window, which had cracked, and proclaimed it unstable; the floor tiles were too uniform to be old. "Imitations," she sniffed.

Sometimes, new employees struggled to fit into the new shops. When a designer pizza place opened, I became acquainted with one of the pizza makers, a young, slim Italian man whose voice had the heavy sound of Sardinia. He knew very little French—but enough to declare many of the pizzas awful, especially the ones with speck and truffle cream. The chemicals used to imitate the flavor of black truffles in what is sold as truffle oil tasted like the metal in the dregs of olive oil tins, he said.

"When the ingredients are really good, you don't need many," he said. "Tomato. Mozzarella. *Basta*. When I go fishing, I go early in the morning, and all I need to do that evening is grill the fish for a minute on each side. *Perfetto!*"

He confessed that he was terribly lonely. I flashed on what my

French tutor at the Alliance Française in Chicago had told me before I moved to France the first time, in 1978.

"Buy a second pillow," I told the pizza guy.

"I don't understand."

"Find a French girlfriend."

"But how do I do that?"

I told him I'd help him work on it. But by the time I returned, he was gone—a fish out of water. He needed the sea. I never even knew his name.

Some closures were inevitable victims of modernity: a DVD rental shop, for example. Yves Hassid, the owner of Paris Video 58, had been on the street for eighteen years. When two other neighborhood DVD shops went out of business, he took over their customers and held on.

Then in June 2013, he posted a sign saying that he, too, was closing. Yves put two large bins holding his stock of DVDs outside the store. Everything was on sale: three euros for run-of-the-mill French comedies, ten euros for classics.

I stopped by on closing day as Yves, all alone, loaded boxes into his car. French law required him to leave the premises clean and empty, as if he had never been there. A sparkly metal Christmas ornament shaped like a stocking hung by a ribbon on the knob of a cabinet. "Compliments of Paris Video" was engraved on the back. It had been a sample made by an advertising promoter who had wanted Yves to put in an order for year-end gifts. Yves is Jewish and celebrates Hannukah, not Christmas, so he never ordered them. But he liked the look of the stocking and kept it. He gave it to me to remember him by. It's corny, but I keep it on my desk as a good-luck charm.

I helped him carry out his boxes. It didn't seem right to end this way, so I said, "Let's have a drink." We walked to the bistro across the street and ordered red wine. Yves cried, just a little.

He left behind his enormous "Paris Video 58" neon sign (No. 58 was his address on the rue des Martyrs). I pleaded with him to keep it as a reminder of his nearly two decades there. I said it was part of his *patrimoine*—that untranslatable French word means heritage, but more than that. He made excuses.

"It's too fragile."

I said we could easily cut away the neon tubes with a wire cutter.

"I don't have a wire cutter."

"I'll go home and get one."

"I didn't negotiate its removal with the new tenant, so it would be illegal."

I gave up.

The sign remained in place for months. Then one day I saw an open door at No. 58. Two young men, a Belgian named Gabriel Mathy and a Norwegian named Viggo Handeland, were discussing plans to open a take-out Belgian waffle shop. I introduced myself and asked if they would save the neon sign.

Sure, they said. They were humoring me, I knew; no way would they make the effort to dismantle and save it. A few months later, Yves's sign was gone, replaced by one that read, "*Le Comptoir Belge—Maître Gaufrier*": The Belgian Counter—Master Waffle Maker.

Not long after, Viggo called me. Did I still want the sign? Did I ever!

I called Yves. I said I had his sign and began to talk logistics. When could he meet me at the shop? When could he bring a car big enough to hold the sign?

Yves was overwhelmed. Words stuck in his throat. He said he had been trying to open a convenience store in the Paris suburb of Asnières-sur-Seine, where he lived, but that he couldn't get the necessary approvals. Convenience shops bring vermin, he was told; they stay open late and attract sketchy people in need of booze.

I told him I would retrieve the sign for him. Trusty Emerik Derian, my former research assistant, immediately hopped on his scooter and met me at the shop. The two men working there were not happy to see us. It was almost five p.m., quitting time. They did not want to hear the story of Yves's sign or Viggo's generosity. But after considerable grousing, they carried it out to the sidewalk.

"Where's your car?" one asked.

I said I didn't have one. He looked at me as if I were insane. Without a word, he returned to the shop and locked the door.

The sign was covered in plaster dust. A small piece of neon from "58" was missing, but otherwise the neon remained firmly attached to its black panel. The panel was bigger than I'd remembered, about four feet tall and five feet wide. Emerik and I tried to lift it. It weighed a ton. Not a ton exactly, but more than we could carry to the bottom of the rue des Martyrs, around the corner, and up a block to my apartment on the rue Notre-Dame-de-Lorette.

Emerik said it would not fit on his scooter. We didn't know where we could borrow a dolly on wheels. We were, however, sure that no taxi driver would be willing to take it. I knocked on the door of the shop. I used my most formal and polite French.

"Excuse me, sir, but we can't lift the sign," I said. "I know this will be an imposition, but would you be so kind as to keep it until my husband can come and take it with our car?"

Even as I said this, I was lying. I had already figured out that the sign would not fit into our car, a very large 1995 Audi A6.

"Lady, you want the sign, you take it," the worker said. "There's no place for it here."

I tried to pull rank. "Your boss wants Monsieur Hassid to have it," I said. "That's why I'm here. It's a surprise for Mr. Hassid. It's part of his *patrimoine*."

By now the workman understood that he was dealing with a lunatic. He offered no help. I told Emerik that, somehow, we had to get the sign home. We began moving downhill on the rue des Martyrs, sliding the huge panel along the sidewalk. We took it slowly, stopping at each curb. As we approached the right turn at the rue Notre-Dame-de-Lorette, I realized it would be a challenge to get the sign into my family's *cave*, our basement storage space.

Karim, one of the street's greengrocers, was having a coffee at the café at No. 8. "Karim, if we get into a real emergency, would you give us a hand?" I asked.

"You can count on me!" Karim said.

Emerik is the most patient young guy I know. He maneuvered the sign into the courtyard of my building and down the narrow, curved stone steps into our *cave*.

That night, I told Andy what I had done. As a lawyer, he wanted the facts, just the facts. How big is the sign? Where exactly did you put it? How did you get it into the basement? How long will it be there?

I was prepared for him to be annoyed. Instead, he said, "It was a *mitzvah*."

Viggo called the next day to ask how the pickup had gone. Instead of telling him the whole story, I said everything was fine. I thanked him again and again. "Newcomers aren't always welcome in the neighborhood," I said. "The old-timers feel they're being pushed out by the young and the rich. And sometimes the new merchants aren't very nice. You did a *mitzvah*, Viggo."

He had no idea what I meant. So I told him that *mitzvah* translates as "commandment" in Hebrew but has come to mean an act of kindness.

"Well, I hope it's just the beginning and I get to do many, many more," he said.

Yves sounded delighted when I phoned with the good news. I told him Andy had called it a *mitzvah*. Yves said he would pick up the sign next day.

"It's much too heavy for one person to carry," I said.

"I'll come with a friend and we'll put it in my car."

I told him it wouldn't fit. He insisted it would.

I told him the neon tube that illuminated the "58" had broken.

Yves was silent. Then he said, "What number 58? Just what did you take?"

"The big sign above the store," I said.

Silence again. He thought I had salvaged a much smaller sign, called a "flag," that juts out perpendicular to the facade, enabling passersby to see a shop's name as they walk up the street—a sign he wanted to rehang if he opened another shop.

"The sign you took is huge!" he said. "It's really heavy. You are crazy! Of course I can't put it in my car. And what am I going to do with it?"

He laughed, but he sounded disappointed.

I apologized for taking the wrong sign. I said maybe he could remove the letters from the wooden frame and hang them on his wall at home—like a piece of modern art.

He talked about the fragility of neon and the challenges of lighting it. Even as he insisted that he wanted the sign, I knew he didn't.

At the new waffle shop, Viggo and Gabriel removed cheap wood flooring to reveal the original nineteenth-century painted tile beneath. They hung a black awning that announced their specialties from the "Belgian Kingdom." They installed a Swiss espresso machine that made Italian caffè macchiato with fair-trade Belgian Taeymans coffee beans, in layers of four colors.

They imported waffle dough from Belgium. Instead of using banal Nutella to make chocolate waffles, the way every other Parisian *crêperie* and waffle maker seems to do, they stuffed theirs with fine Belgian chocolate.

Because apples are emblematic of Belgium, they made fresh-pressed juice from organic apples. They also sold a thick, dark molasses made from apples and pears, Speculoos cookies by the same Speculoos maker that supplies the Belgium royal court, pyramid-shaped raspberry sweets, vanilla cream snowball cookies, and hard salt licorice. Every morning, when they open their window, the fragrance of sugar, butter, and vanilla fills the sidewalk.

Yves, the DVD guy, and his wife, Nathalie, opened the "Looky Caffe" in Asnières-sur-Seine. They chose a solid working-class neighborhood and specialized in what Yves called *la restauration rapide*—fast food. They made salads, sandwiches, and specialties from Tunisia, where Yves was born.

"I've always loved to cook," he said. "I make everything on-site, from scratch."

Yves was reborn.

As for the neon sign, it is still in our *cave* in the basement. Someday, when I live in the United States again, I will hang it in my house as a souvenir of the rue des Martyrs.

LE POTLUCK

...

The sun joyfully taps at your windows;
Love very softly taps at your heart,
And they are both calling you.

—"SOLE E AMORE," GIACOMO PUCCINI

OVER TIME, I GOT TO KNOW SO MANY PEOPLE ON THE
rue des Martyrs that I wanted to bring them together in a celebration of the street—the whole street. But how to do it?

Sébastien! I thought. Sébastien Guénard, the chef and owner of the bistro Miroir, at the top of the rue des Martyrs.

"Imagine a party where everyone comes together," I said. "The people at the bottom meet the people at the top."

"Let's have the party here!" he said.

Miroir used to be a Montmartre joint catering to tourists who craved cheap onion soup and garlicky escargots. Although the place looked filthy and run-down when Sébastien first saw it, it was a *coup de foudre*—love at first sight. "There was a side to the place that said, 'So Paris, the Paris I love, the Paris for real people,'" he recalled.

He opened Miroir in 2008 with financial backing from Bruno

Blanckaert, a businessman with a passion for reviving this part of Paris. Every morning, neighborhood residents stop in for coffee and conversation. The postman comes by, with the mail, of course, but also for a quick espresso; if he is unable to deliver a package to one of the neighbors, he leaves it at Miroir for safekeeping. Because the school nearby bans skateboards, students sometimes leave them with Sébastien until classes let out. Most afternoons, before the restaurant opens for dinner, Sébastien stands on the sidewalk, greeting everyone he knows with double-cheek kisses. Every evening, he sets aside three or four tables for friends and regulars who might show up.

Early some mornings, when I'm not at Le Dream Café, at the bottom of the rue des Martyrs, I venture up here. I perch at a table close to the window and watch the world go by. Catherine Mourrier, a slip of a young woman who chain-smokes and sports a brush cut with her bangs gelled upward, makes me a *café crème* in between washing down the sidewalks and Windexing the windows. She always brings me a small pitcher of extra-hot milk. One day she started serving me croissants.

A man who lives at the top of the street is a different kind of regular. In the old days you would have called him a wino. He carries a guitar on one shoulder and sings when the spirit moves him. He came by one morning and asked Sébastien to open his wine shop, across the street, because he wanted a bottle of red called "Forbidden Fruit." If Sébastien was annoyed, he didn't show it. He unlocked the shop door and handed the man a bottle. The man didn't pay.

"Who was that?" I asked, after he had left.

"An artist of the neighborhood," Sébastien said. "He's as sweet as can be."

"But he didn't pay you!"

"Oh, he'll pay one week or the next."

MY IDEA FOR A party may have seemed whimsical, but I was determined. First, I mentioned it to everyone I knew on the street. Then I hand-delivered invitations. "Dear Martyrians," it began. "The moment I have talked about so much has finally come!" I invited them "to celebrate our rue des Martyrs, which we love so much."

I planned an old-fashioned American potluck dinner. Potluck does not exist in Paris. The French would be unhinged by its disorder: no quality (or quantity) control, no logic to the courses. Even a French family picnic in the country is more formal than an American potluck. To help bring people around, I included a note with the invitation, defining potluck as "a meal in which everyone brings something to eat or drink that can be shared. We do it often in the United States, because it's a great way to meet people around a simple meal."

We needed music, of course. I asked Pablo Veguilla, a young Puerto Rican–American opera tenor, to join us. Pablo is an American success story. He was born poor in Chicago and raised in Orlando, Florida, where his father worked as a nursing home janitor and his mother as a hospital secretary. Yale University plucked him out of oblivion to study music at its graduate school, all expenses paid. He lives with his Romanian-born wife, a pianist, and their three sons, outside of Paris.

"It's not the Met, but we'll have a blast," I said.

I suggested that he sing an aria from Puccini's *La Bohème* because of the opera's historical connection to the Brasserie des

Martyrs, the famous nineteenth-century tavern at the bottom of the street. I told him that Henri Murger, whose book about Paris bohemian life had inspired Puccini, had been a regular there.

"Wonderful! Wonderful!" said Pablo. "I'm getting excited about this."

Most of the shopkeepers I invited shared Pablo's enthusiasm. Arnaud Delmontel, the baker and pastry chef, said he'd bring his signature loaf cakes. His competitor, another Sébastien (Sébastien Gaudard), an even more haute couture baker, promised a surprise. Éric Vandenberghe, the owner of the Corsican food shop, said he'd bring charcuterie. Yves and Annick Chataigner, the cheesemongers, offered Camembert and Beaufort.

But when I asked Guy Bertin, the curmudgeonly bookseller, if he would join us and bring a book, he said, "People don't eat books."

I told him I was planning a raffle as entertainment and we could raffle off one of his books.

"I'm too busy," he said, his voice flat and low.

"It's in the evening, after the shop is closed. Besides, you have to eat."

"I don't go to these things," he said. "Besides, my wife—"

I interrupted: "Bring your wife!"

Nothing is more humiliating than giving a party to which no one comes. So the day before, I made a desperate appeal up and down the street. Abdelhamid and Kamel, the greengrocers, said they couldn't make it.

"If you don't come, I'll be mortified!" I said. "It will be a *vergogna*."

In Italian, *vergogna* is a strong word that means loss of face . . . forever.

I sweet-talked Justine Briolay, whose family had owned La

Poissonnerie Bleue before it closed more than a year before. By this time, Justine knew I was working on a book about the rue des Martyrs. "I am writing this book because of fish," I said. "If it weren't for you and your family's fish store, there wouldn't be a book. You are now the only representative of your family on the rue des Martyrs. Make them proud!"

I knew I had won her over when she sent me a text message asking what to wear.

As for the new fish store, the fishmongers promised to send a delegation.

My friend Amélie Blanckaert, who lives in a house on the rue des Martyrs and whose uncle had helped Sébastien Guénard financially when he started Miroir, called on party day to say she couldn't come. She didn't have a babysitter for her two boys, aged four and two.

"I'll be there in spirit."

"What time do the boys go to sleep?"

"Oh, nine, nine-thirty."

"Bring them! We'll feed them!"

She said she would.

I tried one last time with Guy Bertin. He was wearing a baseball cap and hadn't shaved. He looked awful. "Okay, I'll tell you why I'm not coming," he said. He took off his hat to reveal an ugly sore on his head. "I can't go like this. And it would be impolite to wear a hat."

But he gave me a book, a fine edition of the 1903 novel *Le petit ami* by Paul Léautaud, who had lived on—and written about—the rue des Martyrs.

On party day, I still had not decided what to wear. "No black," my daughter Gabriela said. "Be festive."

I considered red, but Gabriela, who was the designated photographer, nixed that as well. "The walls and banquettes are red, and you would fade into the background," she pointed out.

I decided on a silk print Diane von Furstenberg dress and high-heeled patent leather Louis Vuitton pumps. I had bought both items at Troc en Stock, the secondhand boutique just off the rue des Martyrs. I arrived early at Miroir, giddy and nervous. Sébastien was holding his one-year-old daughter, Automne, in his arms. Pablo, dressed in a black suit, white shirt, and his signature ponytail, was testing an entire sound system he had lugged with him on the hour-long train ride.

"I've got great background music!" he said. "How about Dean Martin?" He mimicked the liquid-smooth croon of the King of Cool. "*C'est si bon*. Lovers say that in France," he sang, then burst into laughter.

Amélie and her sons were the first to arrive; the boys ran around the bistro as if it were their private playground. Within thirty minutes, fifty people had turned up. Just about everyone brought a dish: the baker Sébastien Gaudard, with his Jack Russell terrier on a leash, came with a Saint-Honoré cake (with cream puffs and a mountain of cream) and a Mont-Blanc cake (with pureed chestnuts). He said he could stay for only a few minutes because it was Monday, and Monday was bookkeeping day; he lingered for two hours.

Laurence Gillery, the artisan who repairs barometers, and her mother, Colette, who came all the way from Nice, brought homemade cheese biscuits and a Mediterranean pizza topped with sardines. Makoto Ishii, the manager of the Henri Le Roux chocolate shop, brought a grand box of assorted chocolates and bags of salted caramels. Viggo Handeland, from the Belgian waffle shop, brought three kinds of Belgian cookies. Éric Vandenberghe delivered a three-foot-long platter of Corsican charcuterie. Justine had made a chocolate cake. Didier Chagnas, the retired caretaker at Notre-Dame-de-Lorette Church, had made chocolate mousse.

Thierry Cazaux, the neighborhood historian, brought six copies of his book on the rue des Martyrs. Reilley Dabbs, an American exchange student working with me, brought Oreos. Sébastien Guénard, our host, had made dense meat terrines in large loaves. I brought three of my no-fail potluck salads: rice with tiny cubes of colorful raw vegetables, bow-tie pasta with cherry tomatoes and Pecorino Romano cheese, and curried lentils with golden raisins and pine nuts. On and on went the menu: quiches in different sizes, petits fours in different shapes, sweet and savory cakes.

Wine, lots of it, of course.

Oscar Boffy, the artistic director at the Cabaret Michou, gave Sébastien a Michou apron displaying an image of the cabaret's trademark—the red-lipsticked, long-lashed blond floozy. He gave me a much more precious gift: one of his paintings (he is a painter on the side).

Charmed chaos reigned. We mixed classes and professions: politician, worker, merchant, business executive, writer, artisan, lawyer, retiree, student, artist, and intellectual. Most guests had never socialized with each other before. Some wore dresses and business suits; others came in jeans. Justine had abandoned the black-and-white uniform of the butcher shop, unpinned her bun, and donned colorful print pants, a matching shirt, and lipstick.

Guy Lellouche, the antiques dealer, came in a crisply pressed shirt and velvet slacks, with a silk scarf wrapped twice around his neck and his gray hair dyed brown. Zygmunt Blazynsky, the caretaker at the Saint-Denis crypt, wore a long sheepskin coat that he never removed.

Christophe, the real estate agent, made friends with Viggo, the Belgian waffle guy; Jean-Michel, the Jewish Holocaust survivor, with Didier, the Notre-Dame-de-Lorette Church caretaker; Zygmunt from the crypt with Oscar from Michou.

Jacques Bravo, who had recently retired as the mayor of the Ninth Arrondissement, solemnly proclaimed that by coming to the Eighteenth he had entered foreign territory. "This is a historic moment!" he said. "I have come to Montmartre! I have even dared to come without my passport!"

We packed Miroir so full that Pablo had to perch behind the bar to find a place to set up his sound system. The crowd became silent as he sang the theme song from *The Godfather*, in honor of my Sicilian roots. (We ignored the fact that *The Godfather* is a Mafia movie.) Guy, a classical music buff, didn't know the words, but he "da-da'd" in a voice loud enough for everyone to hear. Passersby gathered outside to listen, and a few tried to push open the door, hoping to join the party.

I called for order. Without success. Finally, Oscar spoke up—in English—in his showman's voice: "Ladies and gentlemen! Please!"

I thanked the crowd for coming to celebrate our street. I told them how much living among them meant to me. "It is impossible for me to be sad on the rue des Martyrs, thanks to you," I said.

"Today, I am living my 'French dream' with you. Of course I am American, of one hundred percent Sicilian descent. But I have to tell you a secret. My mother had blond hair and hazel eyes. Her parents emigrated from Sicily, but they came from . . ."

I hesitated for a second, and Didier Chagnas and Michel Güet both shouted, "Normandy!"

"We're the historian corner!" said Didier. (French schools teach that the Normans conquered southern Italy, including Sicily, in the eleventh and twelfth centuries.)

"So you see, I am really half French!" I said.

"So when are you getting French citizenship, Elaine?" Liliane Kempf called from the crowd.

Pablo led us in Neapolitan love songs and even a tarantella—in Sicilian dialect—before he moved to "Les chemins de l'amour" by Francis Poulenc and then the ultimate French crowd-pleaser, Edith Piaf's "La vie en rose."

At this point, Michel and Didier decided Pablo was just the person to raise money to help restore the crumbling Notre-Dame-de-Lorette Church. They proposed a fund-raiser with him as the star. (They couldn't pay him, of course.) "Maybe a Rossini gala?" they asked.

Pablo suggested Bizet's *Carmen*. He had done his homework and knew that Bizet had been baptized at the church. "*Carmen* brings in the bucks," he said.

Meanwhile, the potluck for fifty was creating a delightful mess at Miroir. Since no one had cut into Sébastien's terrines, I did it myself and served big moist cubes on thin paper napkins. Makoto asked why I hadn't brought out his chocolates, so I set aside the terrines and walked the chocolate box around the room.

At one point we ran out of glasses and dinner plates. I rifled through Sébastien's kitchen cupboards to find more, but they were mostly bare. Some of the guests took turns clearing the tables and washing and recycling the tableware.

By the time I started the raffle, the crowd was deep into food and conversation. I climbed onto a banquette and stood before my guests with odds and ends I had solicited from merchants and residents.

"Is it time for a striptease?" asked Guy Lellouche.

"Very funny," I replied. "Did you know that the modern striptease was invented across the street—at Le Divan du Monde?"

Oscar won a small terra-cotta bell. When he rang it, it emitted a pure, light sound. Oscar is a Buddhist, and the sound pleased him.

Pauline Véron, deputy mayor of the Ninth Arrondissement, won a glass paperweight in the shape of an oversized cut amethyst.

"For the jewel of the rue des Martyrs!" I said as I gave it to her.

I picked up a sixteen-inch, hand-painted porcelain sculpture of Mozart as a young man. To everyone's and no one's surprise, our opera tenor, Pablo, won.

"Ah, it's not possible!" said Liliane Kempf, who had donated it.

"It's perfect!" said Didier.

(Okay, it was fixed.)

Enzo, Sébastien's teenage son, won four recycled books from Circul'Livre, the free book exchange. Jean-Michel Rosenfeld, the retired official from the Jean-Jaurès Foundation, won a photograph of a South African landscape taken by my daughter Gabriela. And so it went, until the crowd lost interest and my voice turned hoarse.

As some guests left, others arrived, including the greengrocers Kamel and Abdelhamid. They brought bananas, apples, and grapes. "I came, Elaine!" said Kamel. He said it again, to make sure I fully appreciated his presence. "Someone asked me to go to a café tonight because I didn't work today, but for you, I came. For you!" Abdelhamid, his father-in-law, stood shyly next to him, smiling and nodding. It was the most touching moment of an emotional evening.

I turned around to see a second Sébastien—the designer pastry chef Sébastien Gaudard. It was time for a random act of meddling. "Kamel, you know Sébastien Gaudard, the best pastry chef of the street? Maybe he could become your client."

The two men shook hands, but they had little to say to each other, and the encounter was stiff. Still, Gaudard needs first-rate fruit for his tarts and sorbets, and Kamel is just across the street. *On ne sait jamais.* You never know.

Two of the young fishmongers arrived, with bottles of sparkling white wine. At close to eleven p.m., the last guest, Raymond Lansoy, the editor of a monthly magazine on Montmartre, appeared. He brought a wine with the unappetizing name: Le Vin de Merde. Everyone thought that was very funny.

Pablo closed the evening with Puccini's "Sole e amore" (Sun and Love), a *mattinata*, or morning song, that first appeared in 1888. He said it was an inspiration for Puccini's *La Bohème,* and he sang:

The sun joyfully taps at your windows;
Love very softly taps at your heart,
And they are both calling you.

Then it was over. I helped Pablo pack up his equipment. "What a great time," he said. "Someone said to me—it was one of the fish guys—that tonight was the first time he ever heard an opera singer. People who didn't know me wanted to talk. People kept saying, 'Let me fix you a plate of food.'

"When you perform onstage, you never see the faces of your audience. Here I was two feet away from the crowd. I could see their reactions. I could hear them humming along. But you know what? People were having such a good time, they didn't need our entertainment to carry the evening."

We lingered, even though it was a Monday night. I stood at the door of the bistro with Sébastien. The evening had been a bigger success than we could have imagined.

"The crazy thing is that everyone came," he said. "People were happy to be here, they were happy to come for the rue des Martyrs. Everyone got involved; everyone brought something, a little present, something to eat.

"And then Pablo! People passing by on the street were amazed to hear an opera singer warming up his voice in a bistro at six p.m. You don't expect to hear an opera singer in a bistro in Montmartre!"

Sébastien was surprised that the informal chaos of the evening had worked so well.

"I'm going to say something awful," he said. "I think we all expected something very American."

"Meaning what?"

"In French people's heads, when you say 'very American,' it's all about the show, the appearance. The people who came tonight know you, so they also know that's not true. But I think they were expecting something much more showoffy, much more bling-bling. But it wasn't at all."

"But, Sébastien, you made it happen!" I said.

"An American party organized by an American in France for French people, with a Puerto Rican–American tenor who sang in Italian," he said. "It was out of this world. You know what I mean? You know what I mean? We had the American melting pot on the rue des Martyrs."

His praise was over the top, but I didn't quarrel with him. When I first came to live in Paris, in 2002, I had hoped to shed my American skin, to become more French. I was set on speaking flawless French with the smoky voice of the actress Jeanne Moreau and on dressing with the insouciance of the perfect Parisienne, Inès de la Fressange. I tried hard to fit in with the rhythm of my former neighborhood off the rue du Bac, in the Seventh Arrondissement, where refinement, restraint, and politesse reigned. It didn't happen. There were just too many codes to master, and the effort that went into it—which should always be invisible—showed through.

On the rue des Martyrs, the codes don't matter. I am embraced because of—not despite—the absence of a glossy French veneer. Authenticity—my identity as an American with deep roots in a foreign land—trumps pedigree.

There is a Sicilian proverb I learned from my father; he learned it from his father: "The shepherd saw Jesus only once." The saying refers to the New Testament story of simple shepherds who were watching their flocks when suddenly angels burst on the scene to announce the birth of Christ. It was a magical moment to be embraced and cherished forever. We may not see choirs of angels, but the proverb is a call to revel in every magical moment. "The shepherd moment" I call it, as corny as it sounds to my kids. And so it was that this night at Miroir was one of those rare moments in life when all seems right with the world.

But it was late. Midnight. Time to go home. Tomorrow would be another day on the only street in Paris.

ACKNOWLEDGMENTS

. . .

O N THE DAY THE SATIRICAL NEWSPAPER *CHARLIE Hebdo* printed its first edition after twelve of its journalists were killed by terrorists in January 2015, I lined up before dawn at the newsagent's shop on the street where I live. I asked to buy twenty copies; Jean-Marc Lépine, the owner, told me there was a quota. He sold me one.

Lépine, like every other newspaper vendor in Paris, sold out quickly. That issue of *Charlie Hebdo* was reprinted, and the next morning, I queued up again. Again, he sold me one copy. The exercise continued, and by the third morning, people standing in line outside the shop were getting to know one another. One woman said she detested the vulgarity of the paper but was buying a copy for her daughter, who had already left for work. One man asked me to hold his place so that he could run over to the rue des Martyrs to buy *chouquette* pastries for everyone in line. There was a lively discussion about the different perceptions of a free press in the United States and France.

There were reminiscences about *Hara-Kiri,* the monthly satirical magazine and predecessor to *Charlie Hebdo.* In the 1960s, *Hara-Kiri*'s offices were located on rue Choron off the rue des

Martyrs. Georges Wolinski, the cartoonist, and Cabu (Jean Cabut), the comic strip artist and caricaturist, had been early contributors to *Hara-Kiri* and longtime staff members of *Charlie Hebdo*. They were killed in the terrorist attack. Their spirits were with us as we waited for the newspaper they believed in.

Meanwhile, Lépine was losing his patience with people who had never bothered to venture into his shop before the *Charlie Hebdo* fever and probably never would again after it subsided. I felt a bit guilty myself. I am one of those dinosaurs who still believe in home-delivery subscriptions—in my case, four daily newspapers and about a dozen weekly and monthly magazines. So I started bringing Lépine small peace offerings: a *pain au chocolat* one day, a bag of clementines the next. On the sixth day of lining up, he handed me a plastic bag with ten copies of *Charlie Hebdo*, and on the seventh day, another plastic bag with another ten.

Such is the spirit in my neighborhood. So my deepest debt in writing this book is to the people who live and work on and around the rue des Martyrs. They shared their stories, welcomed me into their homes and shops, and were never too busy to talk. They gave me lessons: about food, wine, architecture, history, religion, literature, family, secondhand clothing, gilding wood, mouse catching, art restoration, knife sharpening.

Most of all, they gave me their trust.

The idea for the book started small. Susan Edgerley, the wonderful *New York Times* Food editor, assigned me to write a page-long story about the closing of the rue des Martyrs' fish store and its effect on the neighborhood—and on me. I distributed laminated copies of the story to the merchants on the street. They were so enthusiastic that I dared to think big and write more.

My friends came through for me, big-time, as they have in

the past. Susan Fraker, who worked with me at *Newsweek* back in the 1970s, flew to Paris to edit a draft of the book ten days before deadline; we finished in six. Barbara Ireland, a gifted former *New York Times* editor, combed through every line of the manuscript—three times. Jeffries Blackerby, my former editor at the *New York Times*' *T Magazine*, helped shape the manuscript and offered strategic advice. Amy and Peter Bernstein gave it structure at the very beginning. My art historian friend Lin Widmann and my novelist friend Sanaë Lemoine helped with crucial last-minute copyediting. Elisabeth Ladenson gave me a new appreciation for nineteenth-century French literature. Paul Galob provided inspiration laced with humor.

Stephen Heyman, Donna Smith Vinter, Farideh Farhi, Joyce Seltzer, Julia Husson, Geraldine Baum, Maureen Dowd, Carol Giacomo, and Jude Smith were rock-solid pillars of support. My French friends, notably Philippe Hertzberg, Florence Coupry, Bertrand and Marie-Christine Vannier, Bruno Racine, Gérard Araud, Jean-Claude Ribaut, and Abel Gerschenfeld, offered guidance on all things Parisian, from the big to the little. Once again, Ron Skarzenski worked his magic in resolving every technical glitch.

Philip Pullella, a longtime journalist friend from Rome, helped deliver my letter of invitation to Pope Francis. Sébastien Guénard hosted a potluck party at Miroir, his bistro on the rue des Martyrs. Pablo Veguilla, a gifted opera tenor, sang his heart out that night.

Thierry Cazaux, the street's unofficial historian, shared his private collection of old photographs, maps, and prints. Michel Güet and Didier Chagnas were patient and passionate tour guides. Tova Leigh-Choate patiently explained the complicated, convoluted, and conflicting stories about Saint Denis. Reverend

John W. O'Malley, S.J., refined my understanding of Saint Ignatius Loyola and the early Jesuits. Dana Prescott, director of the Civitella Ranieri Foundation in Umbria, Italy, invited me to live and work there among artists, musicians, and writers in the summer of 2014.

Thanks also to Andrew Wylie, my literary agent, and Jeffrey Posternak, his deputy, who once again were faithful, passionate partners in a book project. Jill Bialosky, my editor at Norton, embraced the idea of an offbeat book about a single street with enthusiasm. Bonnie Thompson was a patient, precise copy editor driven by the pursuit of excellence as she improved and corrected the text.

I draw energy from collaborating with young people, and I surrounded myself with several of them, who worked very hard for very little pay. Day after day for a year, Emerik Derian, a brilliant young Renaissance man, was at my side, transcribing interviews, unearthing obscure facts, solving technical problems, and fact-checking. Elizabeth Rosen was a never-take-no-for-an-answer research assistant and a creative mistress of social media.

Marie Missioux, Reilley Dabbs, Benjamin Chaballier, Assia Labbas, Laura Miret, Anne-Louise Brittain, and Ashley Hamill joined up as researchers at various stages, carrying out both routine and impossible assignments. David Broad of Left of Frame Pictures, Cedric Boutin, Benjamin Chaballier, and Naurin Zhang documented life on the rue des Martyrs in video.

As always, the most important support came from my family. My older daughter, Alessandra, played cheerleader from afar, urging me on and telling me jokes. Throughout her life, she has touched me—and just about everyone she meets—with her inner joy. My mother-in-law, Sondra Brown, offered love, support, and hospitality in New York.

My younger daughter, Gabriela, was my visual inspiration. She used her charm and brilliant photographer's eye to coax rue des Martyrians into posing for her. Jean-Michel Rosenfeld opened up his wallet to show her the yellow Jewish star he had been forced to wear during the Nazi Occupation; Oscar Boffy bent the rules and allowed her to photograph Michou's transvestite cabaret show; knife sharpener Roger Henri made a special trip to the street for her. Gabriela's photos capture the spirit of the street through its physical look and its daily life and, most important, through the characters who live and work there. Some are included in the book; others have been published and posted elsewhere.

My husband, Andrew Plump, believed in this book as a way to share the magic of our corner of Paris. He brainstormed about its themes and read the manuscript with lawyerly precision. He shares my excitement for the neighborhood and the rue des Martyrs and, if truth be told, may do more of the food shopping on it than I do. Andy, you are my partner in our long adventure in Paris—and in life.

BIBLIOGRAPHY

. . .

BOOKS

Anglemont, Alexandre Privat d', and Alfred Delvau. *Paris inconnu.* Paris: Adolphe Delahays, 1875.

Apollinaire, Guillaume. *Le flâneur des deux rives.* Paris: Éditions de la Sirène, 1918.

Bangert, William V. *To the Other Towns: A Life of Blessed Peter Favre, First Companion of St. Ignatius.* Westminster, MD: Newman Press, 1959.

Baudelaire, Charles. *Les fleurs du mal.* Paris: Poulet-Malassis et de Broise, 1857.

Bergoglio, Jorge Mario, and Abraham Skorka. *On Heaven and Earth: Pope Francis on Faith, Family and the Church in the Twenty-first Century.* New York: Image, 2013.

Bernheimer, Charles. *Figures of Ill Repute: Representing Prostitution in Nineteenth-Century France.* Cambridge, MA: Harvard University Press, 1989.

Binh, N. T., and Franck Garbarz. *Paris au cinéma: La vie rêvée de la capitale de Méliès à Amélie Poulain.* Paris: Éditions Parigramme, 2005.

Birnbaum, Pierre. *The Idea of France*. Translated by M. B. DeBevoise. New York: Hill and Wang, 2001.

Bowen, Elizabeth. *The House in Paris*. New York: Anchor Books, 1935.

Braudel, Fernand. *The Identity of France*. Vol. 1, *History and Environment*. Translated by Sîan Reynolds. London: HarperCollins, 1990.

Brunel, Pierre. *Rue des Martyrs: Coupeau va mourir en voyant des rats et en criant la soif.* Paris: Les Éditions du Littéraire, 2012.

Buchwald, Art. *Art Buchwald's Paris*. Boston: Atlantic–Little, Brown, 1952.

Burke, David. *Writers in Paris: Literary Lives in the City of Light*. Berkeley: Counterpoint, 2008.

Byrd, Max. *The Paris Deadline*. Nashville: Turner, 2012.

Cantor, Norman F. *Twentieth Century Culture: Modernism to Deconstructionism*. New York: Peter Lang, 1988.

Caraman, Philip. *Ignatius Loyola: A Biography of the Founder of the Jesuits*. San Francisco: Harper & Row, 1990.

Castle, Terry. *The Literature of Lesbianism: A Historical Anthology from Ariosto to Stonewall*. New York: Columbia University Press, 2013.

Cazaux, Thierry. *La cité Malesherbes*. Paris: Paris Musées, 2001.

———. *La mairie du 9e: L'hôtel d'Augny et le quartier Drouot*. Paris: Paris Musées, 2002.

———. *La rue des Martyrs*. Paris: Paris Musées, 2007.

———. *Les boulevards de Clichy et de Rochechouart*. Paris: Paris Musées, 2004.

Centorame, Bruno. *La nouvelle Athènes: Haut lieu du romantisme*. Paris: Action Artistique Ville Paris, 2001.

————. *Le 9e arrondissement: Itinéraires d'histoire et d'architecture*. Paris: Action Artistique Ville Paris, 2000.

Chevalier, Louis. *The Assassination of Paris*. Translated by David P. Jordan. Chicago: University of Chicago Press, 1994.

————. *Les Parisiens*. Paris: Hachette, 1967.

Child, Julia, with Alex Prud'homme. *My Life in France*. New York: Random House, 2006.

Cloarec, Françoise. *Storr: Architecte de l'ailleurs*. Paris: Phebus, 2010.

Cobb, Richard. *Paris and Its Provinces, 1792–1802*. Oxford: Oxford University Press, 1975.

Conrad, Peter. *Modern Times, Modern Places*. New York: Knopf, 1988.

Daudet, Alphonse. *Thirty Years of Paris and of My Literary Life*. Translated by Laura Ensor. London: J. M. Dent, 1902.

Deamer, Dulcie. *The Queen of Bohemia*. St. Lucia, QLD, Australia: University of Queensland Press, 1998.

DeJean, Joan. *How Paris Became Paris: The Invention of the Modern City*. New York: Bloomsbury, 2014.

Deputte, Jocelyne Van. *Vie et histoire du 9e arrondissement*. Paris: Éditions Hervas, 1986.

Descure, Virginie, and Christophe Casazza. *Ciné Paris: 20 balades sur des lieux de tournages mythiques*. Paris: Éditions Hors Collection, 2003.

Dostoyevsky, Fyodor. *The Brothers Karamazov*. Translated by David McDuff. London: Penguin, 2003.

Dumas, Alexandre. *Filles, lorettes et courtisanes*. Paris: Dolin, 1843.

Easton, Malcolm. *Artists and Writers in Paris: The Bohemian Idea*. London: Edward Arnold, 1964.

Eudeline, Patrick. *Rue des Martyrs*. Paris: Éditions Grasset & Fasquelle, 2009.

Fegdal, Charles. *Le neuvième arrondissement: Paris d'hier et d'aujourd'hui*. Paris: Éditions Firmin-Didot, 1939.

Fisher, M.F.K. *Two Towns in Provence: "Map of Another Town" and "A Considerable Town."* New York: Vintage Books, 1964.

Flammarion, Camille. *Discours prononcé sur la tombe d'Allan Kardec*. Paris: Didier, 1869.

Flaubert, Gustave. *L'éducation sentimentale*. Paris: Michel Lévy frères, 1869.

Gabler, James M. *Passions: The Wines and Travels of Thomas Jefferson*. Baltimore: Bacchus Press, 1995.

Gady, Alexandre. *La place Saint-Georges et son quartier*. Paris: Paris Musées, 2003.

Gasnault, François. *Guinguettes et lorettes: Bals publics et danse sociale à Paris entre 1830 et 1870*. Paris: Éditions Aubier, 1992.

Gold, Herbert. *Bohemia: Where Art, Angst, Love, and Strong Coffee Meet*. New York: Simon and Schuster, 1993.

Goldman, Mark. *High Hopes: The Rise and Decline of Buffalo, New York*. Albany: State University of New York Press, 1983.

Goncourt, Edmond, and Jules de. *La lorette*. Tusson: Éditions Du Lerot, 1883.

————. *Journal: Mémoires de la vie littéraire*. 1887–96. Reprint, Monaco: Éditions de l'Imprimerie Nationale de Monaco, 1956.

Gopnik, Adam, ed. *Americans in Paris: A Literary Anthology*. New York: Library of America, 2004.

Grana, Cesar, and Marigay Grana, ed. *On Bohemia: The Code of the Self-Exiled*. New Brunswick, NJ: Transaction, 1990.

Green, Julien. *Paris*. Translated by J. A. Underwood. London: Marion Boyars, 2001.

Hahn, Emily. *Romantic Rebels*. Boston: Houghton Mifflin, 1967.

Harrison, Wilmot. *Memorable Paris Houses*. London: Sampson Low, Marston, 1893.

Hatch, Peter J. *The Fruits and Fruit Trees of Monticello*. Charlottesville: University of Virginia Press, 1998.

Hazan, Eric. *The Invention of Paris: A History in Footsteps*. Translated by David Fernbach. London: Verso, 2010.

Higonnet, Patrice. *Paris: Capital of the World*. Translated by Arthur Goldhammer. Cambridge, MA: Harvard University Press, 2002.

Hillairet, Jacques. *Connaissance du vieux Paris*. Reprint, Paris: Club Français du Livre, 1965.

———. *Dictionnaire historique des rues de Paris*. Reprint, Paris: Éditions de Minuit, 1960.

Holmes, John C. *Nothing More to Declare*. New York: Dutton, 1967.

Horne, Alistair. *Seven Ages of Paris: Portrait of a City*. New York: Knopf, 2002.

Huddleston, Sisley. *Back to Montparnasse: Glimpses of Broadway in Bohemia*. Philadelphia: Lippincott, 1931.

Hussey, Andrew. *Paris: The Secret History*. New York: Viking, 2006.

Jefferson, Thomas. *Garden Book, 1766–1824*. Manuscript. From Massachusetts Historical Society, *Coolidge Collection of Thomas Jefferson Manuscripts*.

————. *The Papers of Thomas Jefferson*. Edited by Julian P. Boyd et al. Princeton: Princeton University Press, 1950.

Johnson, Diane. *Into a Paris Quartier: Reine Margot's Chapel and Other Haunts of St.-Germain*. Washington, DC: National Geographic Society, 2005.

————. *Le Mariage*. New York: Dutton, 2000.

Jones, Colin. *Paris: The Biography of a City*. New York: Penguin, 2006.

Kardec, Allan. *The Spirits' Book*. 1857. Reprint, New York: Cosimo Classics, 2005.

Karnow, Stanley. *Paris in the Fifties*. New York: Times Books, 1997.

Kempf, Bertrand, Liliane Kempf, Laurent Danchin, and Françoise Cloarec. *Marcel Storr*. Paris: Éditions Phebus. 2011.

Klarsfeld, Serge. *Le calendrier de la persécution des juifs en France: 1940–1944*. Paris: Fayard, 2001.

Kock, Paul de. *La grande ville: Nouveau tableau de Paris comique, critique et philosophique*, Vol. 2. Bruxelles: Éditions C. Mucquardt, 1842.

Kronlund, Sonia. *Je me souviens du 9e arrondissement*. Paris: Éditions Parigramme, 2001.

La Bédollière, Émile de. *Le nouveau Paris: Histoire de ses 20 arrondissements*. Paris: Éditions Gustave Barba, 1860.

Lacouture, Jean. *Jésuites*. Paris: Éditions du Seuil, 1992.

La Gournerie, Eugène de. *Histoire de Paris et de ses monuments*. Tours: A. Mame, 1881.

Léautaud, Paul. *Journal littéraire: Juin 1928–février 1940*. Vol. 1. Paris: Mercure de France, 1986.

————. *Le petit ami*. Paris: Mercure de France, 1903.

Lefeuve, Charles. *Histoire de Paris rue par rue, maison par maison*. 5th ed. Paris: C. Reinwald, 1875.

Littlewood, Ian. *Paris: A Literary Companion*. New York: Perennial Library, 1988.

Lottman, Herbert. *The Left Bank*. London: Heinemann, 1982.

Martin, James, S.J. *Between Heaven and Mirth: Why Joy, Humor and Laughter Are at the Heart of the Spiritual Life*. New York: HarperOne, 1989.

————. *My Life with the Saints*. Chicago: Loyola Press, 2006.

Maupassant, Guy de. *Bel-Ami*. Paris: Victor Havard, 1885.

McAuliffe, Mary. *Dawn of the Belle Époque*. Lanham, MD: Rowman & Littlefield, 2011.

Meissner, William. *Ignatius of Loyola: The Psychology of a Saint*. New Haven: Yale University Press, 1992.

Mercier, Louis-Sébastien. *Tableau de Paris*. 2nd ed. 12 vols. Amsterdam, 1783–88.

Miller, Henry. *The Cosmological Eye*. New York: New Directions, 1961.

Moore Whiting, Steven. *Satie the Bohemian: From Cabaret to Concert Hall*. Oxford: Oxford University Press, 1999.

Morel, Dominique. *La nouvelle Athènes: Le quartier Saint-Georges de Louis XV à Napoléon III*. Paris: Paris Musées, 1984.

Mousnier, Roland. *The Institutions of France Under the Absolute Monarchy, 1598-1789, Volume II: The Origins of State and Society*. Translated by Arthur Goldhammer. Reprint, Chicago: University of Chicago Press, 1984.

Murger, Henri. *Scènes de la vie de bohème*. Paris: Éditions Gallimard, 1988.

O'Malley, John W. *The First Jesuits*. Cambridge, MA: Harvard University Press, 1993.

Parry, Albert. *Garrets and Pretenders*. New York: Covici-Friede, 1933.

Paul, Elliot. *The Last Time I Saw Paris.* New York: Random House, 1942.

————. *A Narrow Street.* London: Cresset Press, 1951.

Perec, Georges. *Attempt to Exhaust a Parisian Spot.* Translated by Mary Folliet. Reprint, Black River Falls, WI: Obscure Publications, 1976.

————. *Life: A User's Manual.* Translated by David Bellos. Boston: David R. Godine, 1987.

Powell, Jessica. *Literary Paris: A Guide.* New York: Little Bookroom, 2006.

Priestley, John Boynton. *They Walk in the City.* Leipzig: Tauchnitz, 1937.

Reichl, Ruth. *Remembrance of Things Paris: Sixty Years of Writing from "Gourmet."* New York: Modern Library, 2004.

Rice, Howard C., Jr. *Thomas Jefferson's Paris.* Princeton: Princeton University Press, 1976.

Richardson, Joanna. *The Courtesans: The Demi-Monde in 19th-Century France.* Edison, NJ: Castle, 2004.

Rifkin, Adrian. *Street Noises: Parisian Pleasure, 1900–40.* Manchester: Manchester University Press, 1993.

Russell, John. *Paris.* London: Batsford, 1975.

Seigel, Jerrold. *Bohemian Paris: Culture, Politics, and the Boundaries of Bourgeois Life, 1830–1930.* Baltimore: Johns Hopkins University Press, 1999.

Sempé, Jean-Jacques. *Un peu de Paris.* Paris: Éditions Gallimard, 2001.

Sennett, Richard. *The Conscience of the Eye: The Design and Social Life of Cities.* New York: Knopf, 1991.

Shteir, Rachel. *Striptease: The Untold History of the Girlie Show.* Oxford: Oxford University Press, 2004.

Steward, Rose. *St. Ignatius Loyola and the Early Jesuits.* London: Burns and Oates, 1891.

Tiberi, Jean. *La nouvelle Athènes: Paris, capitale de l'esprit.* Paris: Éditions Sand, 1992.

Toubiana, Serge. *François Truffaut.* Paris: Éditions Flammarion, La Cinémathèque française, 2014.

Vila-Matas, Enrique. *Never Any End to Paris.* New York: New Directions Publishing, 2011.

Wallace, David Foster. *This Is Water: Some Thoughts, Delivered on a Significant Occasion, About Living a Compassionate Life.* London: Hachette UK, 2009.

Weisberg, Gabriel P., ed. *Montmartre and the Making of Mass Culture.* New Brunswick, NJ: Rutgers University Press, 2001.

Wharton, Edith. *French Ways and Their Meaning.* New York: D. Appleton, 1919.

White, Edmund. *The Flâneur: A Stroll Through the Paradoxes of Paris.* New York: Bloomsbury, 2001.

Yans-McLaughlin, Virginia. *Family and Community: Italian Immigrants in Buffalo, 1880–1930.* Ithaca: Cornell University Press, 1977.

Zeldin, Theodore. *The French.* New York: Kodansha America, 1996.

Zola, Émile. *L'Assommoir.* 1877. Translated by Margaret Mauldon. Reprint, Oxford: Oxford University Press, 2009.

———. *The Belly of Paris.* 1873. Translated by Brian Nelson. Reprint, Oxford: Oxford University Press, 2007.

———. *Nana.* 1880. Translated by Douglass Parmée. Reprint, Oxford: Oxford University Press, 2009.

———. *Oeuvres complètes.* Vol. 7: *La République en marche (1875–1876).* Paris: Nouveau Monde Éditions, 2004.

WEBSITES

The Cine-Tourist. "Paris in *Les 400 coups*." http://www
.thecinetourist.net/les-400-coups-paris-locations.html.

Oberg, Barbara B., and J. Jefferson Looney. *The Papers of Thomas Jefferson Digital Edition: Main Series, Volume 8 (25 February–31 October 1875)*. Charlottesville: University of Virginia Press, Rotunda, 2008–2015. http://www.rotunda.upress.virginia .edu/founders/TSJN-01-08-02-0534.

Sand, George. "Letter from George Sand to Eugène Delacroix, October 11, 1846." Musée National Eugène Delacroix. http:// www.musee-delacroix.fr/en/activities-events/recent-acquisitions-41/letter-from-george-sand-to-eugene-delacroix-october-11-1846.

ARTICLES AND ESSAYS

Baudelaire, Charles. "Le peintre de la vie moderne." *Le Figaro* (Paris), November 26, 1863; November 29, 1863; and December 3, 1863.

Bellow, Saul. "My Paris." In *The Sophisticated Traveler: Beloved Cities: Europe*, edited by A.M. Rosenthal and Arthur Gelb, 175. New York: Villard, 1984.

Gautier, Théophile. "Les Lorettes." *Souvenirs de théâtre, d'art et de critiques* (1883).

Thomas, Francis-Noël. "Paris at Street Level." *New England Review* (2009): 152–58.

Wolfe, Tom. "The Saturday Route." In *The Kandy-Kolored Tangerine-Flake Streamline Baby*. New York: Farrar, Straus and Giroux, 1965.

DISSERTATIONS

Leigh-Choate, Tova. "The Liturgical Faces of Saint Denis: Music, Power, and Identity in Medieval France." PhD diss., Yale University, 2009. Ann Arbor: ProQuest/UMI (AAT 3411606).

Sullivan, Courtney Ann. "Classification, Containment, Contamination, and the Courtesan." PhD diss., University of Texas at Austin, 2003.

FILMS

Breakfast at Tiffany's. Directed by Blake Edwards. Paramount Pictures, 1961.

The Da Vinci Code. Directed by Ron Howard. Columbia Pictures, 2006.

The 400 Blows. Directed by François Truffaut. Les Films du Carrosse and Sédif Productions, 1959.

Funny Face. Directed by Stanley Donen. Paramount Pictures, 1957.

Jefferson in Paris. Directed by James Ivory. Touchstone Pictures and Merchant Ivory Productions, 1995.

The Last Metro. Directed by François Truffaut. Les Films du Carrosse, Sédif Productions, TF1 Films Production, Société Française de Production, 1980.

Ratatouille. Directed by Brad Bird and Jan Pinkava. Pixar Animation Studios and Walt Disney Pictures, 2007.

Victor Victoria. Directed by Blake Edwards. Pinewood Studios, 1982.

REPORTS

Brazil's Changing Religious Landscape: Roman Catholics in Decline, Protestants on the Rise. Washington, DC: Pew Research Center, 2013.

2010 Census: Number of Catholics Falls and Number of Protestants, Spiritists and Persons Without Religion Records Increase. Instituto Brasileiro de Geografia e Estatística, November 2010.

SONGS

Aznavour, Charles. "La Bohème." *La Bohème.* EMI, 1996. CD.

Michou. "Moi j'suis Michou." *Michou.* Princess, 1978. 33 rpm.

Paradis, Vanessa. "Mi amor." *Love Songs.* Disques Barclay and Universal Music France, 2013. CD.

Pigalle. "Dans la salle du bar-tabac de la rue des Martyrs." *Un recueil frais et disco.* Az, 2003. CD.